01.06

3 3466 01095 0911

D0852085

JO GARTIN'S
WEDDINGS

An Inspiring Guide for the Stylish Bride

WELD LIBRARY DISTRICT
Greeley, CO   80634-6632

RODALE

Notice

Mention of specific companies, organizations, or authorities in this book does not imply endorsement by the publisher,
nor does mention of specific companies, organizations, or authorities imply that they endorse this book.

Internet addresses and telephone numbers given in this book were accurate at the time it went to press.

© 2006 by Jo Gartin

All rights reserved. No part of this publication may be reproduced or transmitted in any form or by any means,
electronic or mechanical, including photocopying, recording, or any other information storage and retrieval system,
without the written permission of the publisher.

Printed in the United States of America

Rodale Inc. makes every effort to use acid-free ♾, recycled paper ♻.

Book design by Tara Long

Photographs by Joe Buissink, Carin Krasner, and Elizabeth Messina

Photograph on page 112 by Tara Rochelle; photograph on page 115 by Liz Banfield

Library of Congress Cataloging-in-Publication Data

Gartin, Jo.
    Jo Gartin's weddings : an inspiring guide for the stylish bride.
        p.   cm.
    Includes index.
    ISBN-13 978–1–59486–261–8 hardcover
    ISBN-10 1–59486–261–3 hardcover
    1. Weddings—Planning. 2. Wedding etiquette. I. Title: Weddings. II. Title.
HQ745.G36 2006
395.2'2—dc22   2005030246

Distributed to the book trade by Holtzbrinck Publishers

2 4 6 8 10 9 7 5 3 1 hardcover

We inspire and enable people to improve their lives and the world around them

For more of our products visit **rodalestore.com** or call 800-848-4735

love

honor

these words are written
with love for
christopher and sydney

kiss

cherish

happiness

luck

celebrate

contents

A HUGE THANK YOU

TO MY AGENTS, JENNIFER RUDOLF-WALSH AND ANDY MCNICOL, FOR HELPING THIS BOOK BECOME EVERYTHING I IMAGINED. TO MY INSPIRING EDITOR, LEIGH HABER, FOR EMBRACING MY VISION AND TURNING IT ALL INTO A REALITY. TO TARA LONG AND THE ART DEPARTMENT AT RODALE FOR DESIGNING SUCH PERFECT PAGES. TO MY AMAZING PHOTOGRAPHERS, JOE, CARIN, AND ELIZABETH: IT WAS AN ABSOLUTE HONOR TO WORK WITH YOU. TO KIMBERLY AND MARCELA FOR YOUR TIRELESS HELPING HANDS. TO DARA ROCHELLE FOR LENDING YOUR CULINARY GENIUS. TO THE OUTRAGEOUSLY TALENTED MONIQUE LHUILLIER AND YOUR ADORABLE STAFF FOR WELCOMING ME INTO YOUR WORLD OF BREATHTAKING DESIGNS. TO CLAUDE MORADY JEWELERS FOR YOUR EXQUISITE DIAMONDS. TO JESUS AT TOPOZIOS CAKE ARTISTRY FOR YOUR DIVINE TOWERS OF SUGARY PERFECTION. TO DAVID'S BRIDAL FOR ALLOWING ME TO ADD MY TOUCH TO YOUR GOWNS. AND TO MY BEAUTIFUL FAMILY AND FRIENDS FOR THE GIFT OF HAVING YOU ALL IN MY LIFE!

dear miss bride-to-be,

Congratulations! You are about to plan the ultimate celebration of love. I can vividly remember standing in your shoes. My husband proposed to me in the pouring rain on a boat on the Hudson River with the Statue of Liberty watching over us. Suddenly, I had this beautiful sparkle on my left ring finger and images of my wedding day floating around in my imagination. But back then, I was not in the business of planning events. I was just your typical bride conjuring visions of her dream wedding. Our budget didn't allow for a coordinator or a designer, and so I was forced, though very willingly so, to dive headfirst into the world of weddings. I looked high and low for inspiration, searching out all the publications pertaining to planning, budgets, and checklists. But what I really wanted was a book filled with unique ideas, a book that would help me make my wedding wonderful!

Planning a wedding can be a fun, even an amazing, journey. I've taken it myself as a bride, and now I do it for a living as an event coordinator and designer. I absolutely love what I do. Each event allows me to embark on a sort of creative escapade. I relish searching for fabulous finds. I love having to be resourceful and practical. And I really hate to be ripped off. I've discovered that attention to detail is essential, and I am absolutely dedicated to creating that "wow" factor we all hope to achieve, only in my case I'd prefer it to be "Wow! That's so original "as opposed to "Wow, they must have spent a fortune. "I am addicted to perfection and am a believer that presentation can be everything. I enjoy taking elements of tradition and then adding my own special twist. But above all, I think small personal touches are really the key to creating memorable weddings; these are the flourishes that let you showcase your individual style, and at the same time are the essence of thoughtfulness.

In the coming pages, I am delighted to share with you my unique ideas, personal touches, savvy secrets, and helpful hints. From stationery and flowers, through food presentation and keepsakes, I will offer you a variety of fresh ways to impress. I'll give you some of my tricks of the trade, little secrets that I've used in my favorite magazine spreads, and little glimpses into some celebrity celebrations I've coordinated. Consider me your fairy godmother! My gift to you is a compendium of wedding inspiration, stylishly wrapped and brimming with ways to make your wedding wonderful.

wishing you love, luck, and angels,

let's get this party started!

He proposed and you said yes!

So let the celebrations commence. **You're officially engaged,**

and I'm guessing you're already being hit with the questions:

Have you set the date? Where will you be married? Who made the guest list?

Will you wear white? What are the colors? What is your budget?

A little overwhelmed? Well, I can't make all the busybodies disappear,

but I can offer my experience to help you make your wedding special.

PLANNING, BUDGETS, CHECKLISTS PLEASE

I initially toyed with the idea of creating a step-by-step guide to planning your wedding, which would cover topics like budgeting and etiquette. But these areas have all been well covered by others, and so I opted instead to write something a little more personal. I have sprinkled a handful of little planning tips throughout, but my focus is on presenting you primarily with ideas. Bookstores seem to be overflowing with wedding books offering checklists and budget planners and wedding planning ABCs. And a lot of this information is readily available at no cost on wedding Web sites such as theknot.com.

In any case, I feel it is incredibly difficult to generalize in these areas, as each couple is unique in their circumstances and the amount of money they have to spend on their special day. Priorities also vary considerably. I have clients who spend thousands on a band while others prefer to go with a DJ. Some couples are real foodies, while others would rather focus on getting creative with the cocktails. Some clients order invitations that double as gifts, while others choose more traditional stationery. I can't make these decisions for you. They are purely personal—there is no right and wrong, though I do advise that you make a list of your priorities so that you can decide how to allocate your budget.

DREAM, DREAM, DREAM— CAPTURING YOUR VISION

I'm not sure if you grew up dreaming of wearing a billowing ivory gown at your wedding by the sea, but whatever it is, I think every event should begin with an overall vision. This inspiration can stem from your *personal style*, a favorite *color palette*, your desired *décor*, the array of *flowers* you imagine gracing your tables, *traditions, including those involving the menu*, or most commonly, the *location* you prefer.

Personal Style

You may love the intricacy of the formal English style and desire eclectic silver julep cups and engraved bone china surrounded by full-bloomed ranunculus. You might also admire the simplicity of a wedding in a modern loft, or, alternatively, romantic nuptials framed by a rustic ranch. Well, unless you have a few days and a lot of spare cash, it's not likely that you can have them all—and certainly not all in the same place, unless you want your wedding to resemble a carnival more than a celebration of love.

   If your style is more contemporary, you may be happiest having your wedding in a museum or under a tent that you treat as a blank canvas and decorate to make your own. If you love the beach, you may want to exhaust all possible seaside locations before deciding on something else, but I suggest you don't rule out other venues at the start. You may be surprised what you might fall in love with. It tends to be difficult to settle on only one style for your wedding and wave good-bye to the rest, but it is almost impossible to move forward without doing so.

it pays to prioritize

Take a moment to rank each element of your wedding in order of importance to you. Determining what is most important will help you distribute your budget accordingly. Here are the key components that I refer to when outlining priorities with my clients.

Beverages
Bridal gown and accessories
Celebrant
Coordinator
Favors
Flowers
Food
Hair and make-up
Honeymoon
Insurance
Location
Music
Photography
Rentals
Specialty linens
Stationery
Styling and décor
Transport
Valet
Videography or cinematography
Wedding cake
Welcome gifts

consider colors

Your wedding can simply be planned around your favorite colors. I often let color dictate my design. Let's peek at my most popular wedding color palettes.

Layers of Latte

This neutral color palette is made up of varying shades of taupes and browns. Blush pink is a perfect accent color. Deep burgundies and reds match perfectly, and terra-cotta introduces a rustic warmth. You may also like to consider copper, bronze, or silver accents. I have also designed exclusively within these neutral shades, using curly willow branches, pinecones, and dozens of candles with a few ivory blooms as accents. For one winter wedding, coffee even became a theme—tables were named after grinds of coffee, and welcome bags with Starbuck's frappuccinos and cappuccinos made perfect take-home treats.

Celebrate in Celadon

These calming shades of pale green are my most requested color palette. They hold up wonderfully on their own and provide a perfect base for accent colors such as fuchsia pink, dusty rose, oranges, and deep reds. You can add earthy components such as curly willow branches and dried artichokes or introduce formality with elegant silver urns and julep cups overflowing with fragrant ivory garden roses and antique hydrangeas. Invitations in these shades can be as classic as they can be modern. Add green to your stationery by letter pressing or printing in celadon or feature a pressed cloverleaf accent (available at www.pressedflower.com).

Chocolate Craving

I think it's true that brown is the new black! You may like to add a subtle twist to your classic stationery and print in chocolate brown instead of black. This particular color palette was used for a spring wedding. The flowers were pale pink cherry blossoms arranged in chocolate Balinese wooden vases, and the bride carried a bouquet of hand-wired pale pink cymbidium orchids. The polka-dot ribbon sealed the welcome gifts waiting in each guest's hotel room, tied the napkins at the dining tables, and knotted the bags of doughnut holes we offered as a midnight snack. Chocolate and powder blue is also a popular combination as is brown and red and browns with shades of rust.

Green with Envy

An all green and white color palette is one of my favorites—it has a freshness to it. Choose varying shades of rich green fabric and ribbons, or search for the perfect patterned fabric and tie that in by making custom table runners, seat-cover ties, or napkins, for example. Having custom napkins made at a local alterations place is often the same price as specialty rentals. This way you get totally original napkins, and you'll have a lifetime supply of them for your dinner parties to come! Giant elephant leaves, lily grass, potted succulents, cacti, citrus cymbidium orchids, garden herbs, and berries are some of my favorites to use for centerpieces.

Earthy Elements

Incorporating textures adds dimension to your color palette. Introduce woven straw ribbons as accents for welcome boxes or favors, for example. Handmade earthy papers are a great complement for stationery items. Choosing a neutral base welcomes a variety of complementary accent colors. Ruby red roses overflowing from dark wooden boxes or arrangements of tropical leaves and fuchsia pink can be striking. I have also added branches of winterberries to these earthy shades. A mix of all-white flowers could be stunning—add accents of delicate chocolate cosmos or burgundy dahlias to the white blooms for a bold contrast.

Tangerine Twist

I think orange signifies happiness. Consider adding touches of tangerine throughout your stationery, too—maybe an orange outer envelope or a pressed tangerine daffodil accent. (I order my pressed leaves and flowers from www.pressedflower.com.) One of my favorite fall weddings had giant arrangements of orange Singapore orchids atop banquet tables set with ivory linens and bamboo table runners. For a fun touch, treat your bathrooms to a giant bowl of goldfish!

White on White

This quintessential wedding palette of shades of white is timeless. Combine velvet and fur for a wintery feel or linens and chiffon for a celebration in the summer. Keep it traditional with antique silver urns filled with roses and gardenias, or pot giant white orchids in oversize vases lined with white river rocks for a modern edge. If you are walking down the aisle in a lace gown, you may like to tie that in to your celebration—use a lace flower on your invitation, line the base of your wedding cake with lace, or wrap lace around your bouquets. Shades of white and ivory invite almost any accent color, such as chocolate brown, canary yellow, fire engine red, or others.

Décor

Whether you want to hang silk lanterns, rent velvet chaise longues for a cocktail hour, or add an Asian twist with walls lined with bamboo, look for a space that accommodates. For example, a hotel ballroom might not be the best setting for your lanterns, but it may be ideal for a lounge theme.

Flowers

Sometimes flowers can be a determining factor in choosing your theme. The seasons play a part here. For example, one of my brides insisted on having peonies at her wedding. This meant that a fall wedding was out of the question, as peonies are almost impossible to find during the fall months.

Maybe you are in love with a particular flower. If it's red roses that take your fancy, then you may decide to decorate with warm jewel tones and rich velvets. Alternatively, I think the sharp contrast of ruby reds against crisp whites is just amazing.

If you love orchids and the more modern tropical blooms, then search for a space that complements and sets off their special flair. For example, picture orchids in an airy loft, ginger flowers at a museum of contemporary art, or hundreds of succulents at a seaside celebration.

Honoring Heritage

Maybe you'd like to incorporate your family heritage or certain elements of family traditions. I served a dessert of fresh lemon crepes to represent one bride's French lineage. Mississippi mud cakes and Boston cream pies have also made appearances on my clients' lists of sweet treats.

If you are Italian, you might like to recreate a Tuscan setting with a family-style banquet at long tables scattered with assorted authentic Chianti bottles and clusters of candles. You may even like to serve numerous smaller courses with a special tasting of wine with each—think of it as an elaborate wine-tasting wedding!

Or why not embrace your Hindu ancestors by holding your ceremony underneath hanging garlands of marigolds? Then, for the reception, treat guests to an Indian feast displayed along tables dressed in traditional saris. Serve chai and lassis with your wedding cake.

The setting of your wedding will obviously play an enormous role in establishing your overall aesthetic. You may have had your heart set on a beach ceremony laced with giant sunflowers, but you may surprise yourself and fall in love with a vineyard, in which case sunflowers may not work. So whether you've dreamt of a Spanish wedding drenched in jewel-toned roses, or imagined an elegant Balinese cocktail party beneath a sky of brightly colored silk lanterns, you will need to coordinate the feel of your wedding with the venue itself, and ensure that they are complementary. I find examples can be a great help. Let me put into words the atmosphere I have created for some of my clients . . .

Wed in the Winter. For a winter wedding I chose shades of brown and splashes of red. I designed an outdoor tent (this was in California) draped overhead in luxurious chocolate brown velvet and hung decadent crystal chandeliers from the peaks. The flooring was ivory carpeting layered in fresh crimson rose petals. Guests dined at banquet tables (these are just long tables as opposed to round) set with cappuccino linens and chocolate brown woolen table runners. The flower arrangements were hand-opened shades of blood red roses ('Black Magic' and 'Intuition') arranged in modern square glass vases that I lined with rose petals. Following an exquisitely prepared dinner of hazelnut-crusted filet mignon, guests were invited to the dessert lounge—where trays of bite-size desserts (the tiramisu served in espresso cups with demi spoons were my favorite) were waiting alongside an antique cappuccino bar complete with personalized mugs of old-fashioned hot chocolate and king-size vanilla marshmallows.

Put Some Spring in Your Step. A recent spring bride adored butterflies, so I subtly added delicate butterflies made from feathers to her garden celebration. I hung them from the trees that encircled the outdoor dining room, and I tucked them into her French tulip centerpieces. The menu complemented the lush green surroundings. Watermelon lemonade and assorted mini tea sandwiches greeted guests on arrival. Guests enjoyed mint cucumber soup shots and tuna sashimi cornets, among other cocktail appetizers. Citrus-infused grilled lobster tails and leek and celery ravioli were offered as a main course . . . and as a tribute to the groom's hometown, we served individual Key lime tartlets for dessert.

Say I Do in the Summer. A summer wedding in a downtown L.A. loft called for modern elegance. The color palette consisted of a terrain of greens. Oversize vases were filled with towering curly willow and giant elephant palms. Celadon cymbidium orchids and assorted berries graced the dining tables. I designed a menu with an Asian twist and had lychee and raspberry soju butler-passed throughout the evening.

Walk down the Aisle in Autumn. A fall celebration invited a rust-colored palette. The venue was a hotel ballroom. I hung sheer taupe drapes down the walls of the room to create a giant living room feel. Tables were set using the hotel's ivory linens. I chose napkins (not from the hotel) in a fabulous mocha silk and paired them with an elegant menu and an autumn maple leaf accent from the mother-of-the-bride's garden. Centerpieces were arranged in custom wooden boxes that the bride stained herself in an afternoon with a few friends. I used hints of berries, pinecones, and acorns to embrace the fall, and guests dined on roast chestnut soup served in hollowed-out baby pumpkins, apricot-glazed rack of lamb, and assorted baked squash. Pecan pie and fresh whipped cream topped off the menu.

Memories of Morocco. A Moroccan feast served family-style in a grand old castle was a spectacular sight. I set banquet tables with linens in rich tones of merlot and copper and lined them with an authentic gold and silver overlay (I rented these from a local Moroccan store). Centerpieces boasted assorted crimson blooms tucked into mismatched Moroccan teapots, and tea lights illuminated traditional Moroccan tea glasses. After dinner, guests lounged on rugs and cushions scattered about oversize coffee tables stacked with delicious desserts and sweet Moroccan mint tea. Twelve belly dancers serenaded the newlyweds with a magnificent performance that left the guests speechless.

Hold onto Hollywood. A private home with an old Hollywood feel called for an art deco edge. Peacock feathers made subtle appearances. Old black and white movies were projected on walls throughout the cocktail lounge, and after guests had worn out their dancing shoes, we invited them to relax in a private screening room filled with throw pillows and rugs where we played a mini movie put together by the groom's brother. Friends had collaborated to recreate special moments of the bride and groom's relationship—in true comedic fashion. Popcorn, red vines, and Raisinets were in plentiful supply, along with old-fashioned bottles of Jones soda with a personalized photo label of the cinema where the couple had their first date. You can order these personalized sodas through their Web site, www.myjones.com.

The Perfect Picnic. On a giant lawn overlooking the ocean, I set up elegant picnic tables dressed in chocolate gingham linens. Potted daffodils were placed in the center of each table, and for lunch we set up an incredible mix of carving stations offering gourmet sandwiches, roasted corn on the cob, baked potatoes, and assorted summer salads. Guests were invited to dine barefoot, and after lunch, in place of daytime dancing, traditional games of croquet were played. The take-home favors were small picnic baskets filled with jars of delicious homemade treats.

Reminiscing on the weddings I've helped create enables me to present you with some of my favorite touches. You may not have access to such things as a private screening room (not many of us do), but the concepts are there waiting to be adapted. For example, you might like to set up a mini movie theater at your venue using a projector and a huge screen. Or, renting flat-screen TVs could be another option. I look forward to sharing other memorable moments with you in the pages to follow.

With your location set and the overall style of your celebration decided upon,

the planning can really move forward. And I often think securing your venue

is the most challenging component, so please don't be disheartened

if you're feeling a little anxious at this stage. It all tends to be downhill from here.

So slip on some comfortable shoes and enjoy the ride.

stationery stories

Invitations often have the delightful job of introducing your celebration. I loved this element of weddings so much that I launched my own stationery collection.

My goal for the invitations I create is to capture each couple's personal fairy tale, which means that every design should be one-of-a-kind. I love to imagine each recipient opening the envelope in anticipation of its contents. Knowing I helped launch that initial wedding day buzz is so rewarding.

Selecting your wedding stationery can be a little tougher than you might anticipate. After all, it's often not just the invitation you are choosing; it can also include save-the-date cards, programs, menus, escort cards, place cards, welcome notes, thank you notes . . . basically everything that gets printed! Of course, you don't necessarily need all of these items. Take programs, for example. Many couples I've worked with like having a printed itinerary for their ceremony. This is often a nice addition, but it's certainly not mandatory.

You might try beginning your stationery adventure by writing a list of all of the paper components in order from your "must haves" through to "not really needed." Since this boils down to personal preference, there is no such thing as "good grades" for this task, so have fun. With your homework out of the way, we can start looking at great ways to personalize your wedding stationery.

PLEASE SAVE OUR DATE

It has become increasingly popular for couples to formally announce their wedding day by mailing out a save-the-date card. This gives out-of-town guests plenty of time to make the necessary travel arrangements, and if you are planning a destination wedding, it is the perfect opportunity to enclose travel information details. Again, you do not have to opt for save-the-dates. You may decide to choose a less formal way of letting your guests know your plans, whether by phone call or via a save-the-date e-mail.

I approach every save-the-date differently. Will you keep yours classic and simple, or do you want to have a little more fun with it? Remember, your decisions are yours to make. Keeping all of your stationery items consistent in terms of colors and style is the way to play it safe. But there is absolutely no reason why you can't send a fun save-the-date and then follow with a more formal invitation. I like to design save-the-dates with a bit of a twist. Here are some of my favorites.

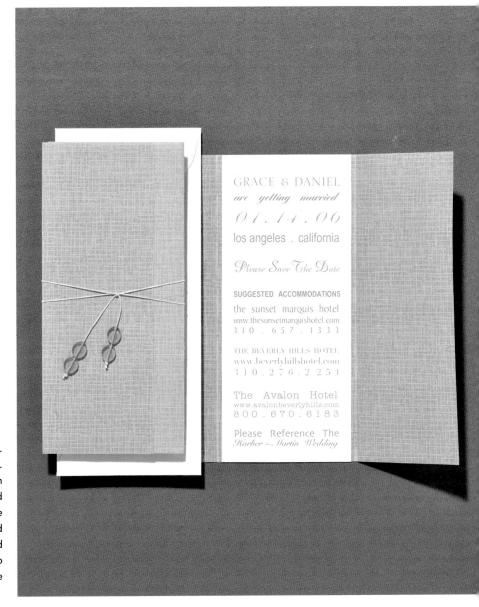

begin with beads

This is one of my most popular designs. It has a very elegant, yet modern edge. This save-the-date is offset printed on two-ply European museum board and then affixed to and wrapped in sage green textured opaque vellum. I secured it with oatmeal waxed twine and added four resin bead accents (be sure to choose flat beads so they don't buckle your envelope when inserted).

GRACE & DANIEL
are getting married
01.14.06
los angeles . california

Please Save The Date

SUGGESTED ACCOMMODATIONS
the sunset marquis hotel
www.thesunsetmarquishotel.com
310 . 657 . 1333

THE BEVERLY HILLS HOTEL
www.beverlyhillshotel.com
310 . 276 . 2251

The Avalon Hotel
www.avalonbeverlyhills.com
800 . 670 . 6183

Please Reference The
Harber ~ Martin Wedding

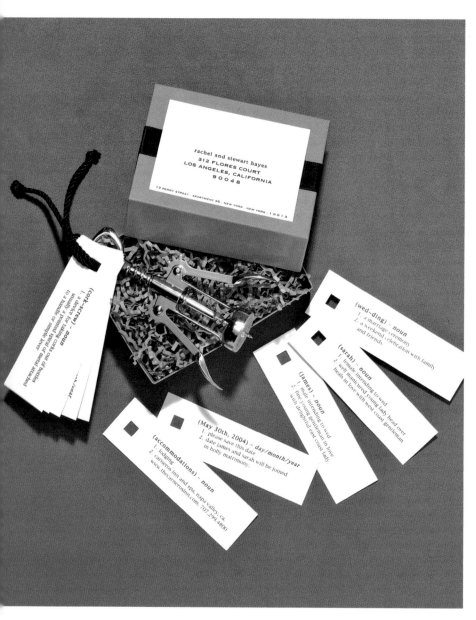

box the date

Receiving a save-the-date in a box makes for a great first impression. My three-dimensional save-the-dates have become very popular. For a Napa Valley wedding I planned, guests opened a kraft paper box secured with crimson satin ribbon to find inside a corkscrew wine opener attached to a booklet revealing the wedding details. They were written like Oxford dictionary definitions but paired with my own invented meanings about the couple's courtship. Wasn't this perfect for a wedding set in a vineyard? And I think everyone wishes they had an extra corkscrew at some point or another. (Some post offices require you to seal boxes with packing tape instead. In these cases, I use kraft paper tape. It's wise to check with your local post office beforehand.)

KATE & MAX
ARE GETTING
MARRIED
07.03.05
EAST HAMPTON
NEW YORK
PLEASE
SAVE THEIR DATE

save-the-date cards —literally!

This personalized deck of playing cards is printed on heavy card stock. It is tied with waxed twine and mailed in either a rectangular kraft paper box or a "traditional" red envelope. You might also like to put the cards in a plastic case and mail them in a box. (If you decide on an envelope, I recommend choosing a padded one.) Adding poker chips with your names and your wedding date is a cute touch. To order, search online for personalized playing cards and personalized poker chips.

the day
they met

SEPTEMBER
TWENTY FOURTH
2 0 0 2

ALISON
❋ ❋
JEFFERY

a love story

An always adorable mini album (available in various colors at www.kolo.com) can highlight a handful of the couple's most memorable dates or moments leading up to the wedding day. This one started with the day the couple met and ended with the date they were asking each guest to save (i.e., the wedding date!). I accented each mini album with a strand of colorful ribbon and mailed it in a square envelope large enough to travel through the post.

MICHELLE

&

OLIVER

Are Delighted to Announce
Their Upcoming Wedding

PLEASE SAVE THEIR DATE

0 2 . 0 2 . 0 4
. . .

IN THE HILLS
HOLLYWOOD, CALIFORNIA

Details to Follow

---

on october eighth
two thousand and five
in their hometown
of seattle, washington

CATE
ROBERTS
and

JOHN
KNIGHT

Will Say 'I Do'

PLEASE
SAVE
THE
DATE

for wedding details
and recommended
accommodations
please visit
www.johnlovescate.com

TESSA BRENT

A Wedding Celebration

THE PHILLIPS AND THOMPSON FAMILIES ARE EXCITED
TO ANNOUNCE TESSA AND BRENT'S UPCOMING SUMMER NUPTIALS.
NOVEMBER FIFTH . TWO THOUSAND & FIVE . SANTA BARBARA . CALIFORNIA

PLEASE SAVE THE DATE

FOR ACCOMMODATIONS PLEASE MENTION THE PHILLIP~THOMPSON WEDDING

THE FOUR SEASONS	MONTECIETO INN	EL ENCANTO
805.969.2261	800.843.2017	805.687.5000
www.fourseasons.com	www.montecitoinn.com	www.elencantohotel.com

---

This handful of samples from my stationery portfolio offers examples of how wording, typeface (fonts), and layout can have an impact on your save-the-dates.

There is no strict rule for how far in advance to mail a save-the-date card. If there is a long-distance travel component, then obviously, the earlier the better. But don't go to the extreme—mailing them 18 months ahead of time may be a little too early, and you don't want people to forget! By the same token, if you have only 2 or 3 months to go before your big day, sending a save-the-date card may be redundant. In that case, you should probably just send out your invitation as early as you can and include any travel details with it.

A Couple More Save-the-Date Ideas

Postcards. Postcards are a sweet and cost-effective way to announce your date. Here are some hints for creating a memorable postcard.

- ✦ Use a favorite photograph, maybe of your wedding location. You might even like to try using your photographic talents behind the camera . . .

- ✦ Feature a poem or the story of how you met.

- ✦ Add a twist and create a round or square postcard.

- ✦ Be sure your save-the-date will stand out among all of the junk mail we receive on a daily basis!

Save-the-Date CD. Send your save-the-date in audio form by recording a personal message for your guests on a CD. Tell a little story of your engagement or try serenading each other, for example—along with telling your guests when and where the wedding will be held, of course. Add humor or keep it sweet and heartfelt—or try a combination of the two. Either way, recording this CD should be a lot of fun. The Web sites www.beau-coup.com and www.myownlabels.com are great places to order CD packaging and personalized CD labels.

Scroll It. Scroll your save-the-date and mail it in a post office approved canister. You might like to tie it with ribbon or string or seal it using sealing wax for an old-fashioned feel.

Save-the-Date Sachet. For a garden wedding, affix printed labels to sachets of seeds from your favorite herbs or flowers. (Note that overseas mailings may have customs issues.)

INVITATIONS TO IMPRESS

Every couple is different in terms of the level of importance they place on their invitations. Classic calligraphy could be perfect for your celebration. Maybe something with a modern flair is more your style, or you could be in search of something wholly original that has never been done before. My custom designs tend to be a little more stylized—on the following pages, you can take a peek into my personal portfolio.

Sending a Scent

Tap into the senses. Your guests should be impressed by what they see when they open your invitation—but why not treat their sense of smell, too? Before placing each invitation in its envelope, gently spritz it with your favorite scent. (I find that room spray works well, too.) Before you scent all your invitations, though, do a test by spraying one invitation and letting it set for a day—check to be sure your stationery doesn't discolor or have some other reaction to your fragrance.

spell-check

Be sure to carefully fact-check and spell-check all of your printed material before giving your approval to print. It helps to have a couple of sets of eyes look it over for you.

postage pointers

It is wise to visit your local post office with a sample of your save-the-date and invitation to make sure they approve of the packaging and that you have the correct postage. For three-dimensional invitations, some post offices require that you seal boxes with packing tape, in which case I use a brown tape that requires moisture to adhere.

Square and odd-shaped envelopes require additional postage. I am always careful to separate overseas mailings and ensure that they have correct postage and any necessary customs forms (typically required for three-dimensional invitations).

<![CDATA[
she said seashells

This beach celebration was introduced with a kraft paper square box housing a letter-pressed contemporary invitation affixed to and wrapped in frayed-edged sage burlap. The invitation was then accented with ivory twine tied to a seashell and placed in a box, which was sealed using olive green grosgrain ribbon and an address label.

MR. & MRS. JOHN TOWN
83254 CORONA DEL MAR
PACIFIC PALISADES, CALIFORNIA
9 0 2 7 2

8426 CAMDEN DRIVE · BEVERLY HILLS · CALIFORNIA · 90210

AFTERNOON

at sunset
on the coast of mexico

CORRIE SAFRIS
&
KEN NOLAN

together with their families
invite you to celebrate their marriage

saturday
at half past four
0 2 . 1 9 . 0 5

on the beach
palmilla resort
cabo san lucas, mexico

cocktails, dinner
and dancing to follow

festive attire

for information
on the golf course
please check out
www.cabodelsol.com
]]>

about bamboo

These invitations were originally designed for Taye Diggs and Idina Menzel's Jamaican celebration. They were also featured on the *Today* show. Believe it or not, I simply affixed this invitation to a custom-cut sushi mat using craft glue. Each invitation and RSVP card was then accented with a pressed daffodil flower. It was very labor intensive but will seem well worth the effort when your guests all call to express their delight.

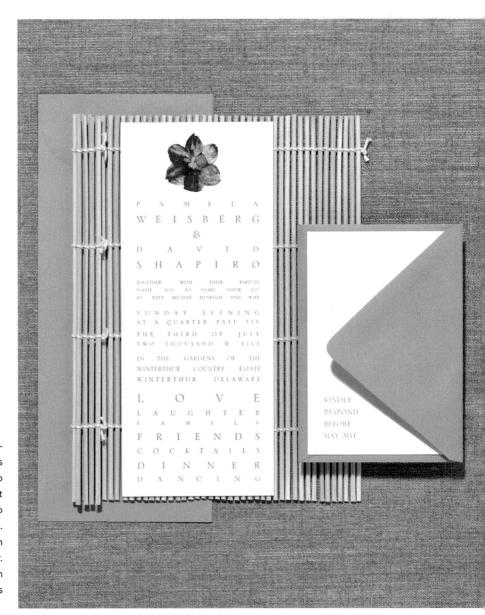

PAMELA
WEISBERG
&
DAVID
SHAPIRO

TOGETHER WITH THEIR PARENTS
INVITE YOU TO SHARE THEIR JOY
AS THEY BECOME HUSBAND AND WIFE

SUNDAY EVENING
AT A QUARTER PAST SIX
THE THIRD OF JULY
TWO THOUSAND & FIVE

IN THE GARDENS OF THE
WINTERTHUR COUNTRY ESTATE
WINTERTHUR DELAWARE

LOVE
LAUGHTER
FAMILY
FRIENDS
COCKTAILS
DINNER
DANCING

KINDLY
RESPOND
BEFORE
MAY 31ST

mosaics

Designing these invitations was a true labor of love. These original art pieces were made using hand-cut shards of opaque glass. Then I mounted the invitations, which were printed on a latte-colored card stock, on the other side. Once all the wedding details were noted, guests were able to enjoy the invitation as a wall hanging.

IT IS WITH GREAT JOY
AND EXCITEMENT THAT

Penelope McKnight

&

Harrison Eggert

INVITE YOU TO CELEBRATE
THEIR MARRIAGE

SATURDAY AFTERNOON
AT HALF PAST FOUR
THE SIXTEETH OF OCTOBER
TWO THOUSAND AND THREE

TEHAMA GOLF CLUB
CARMEL, CALIFORNIA

ELEGANT ATTIRE

invitation unfolded

I love this invitation. I have designed many variations and always receive such nice compliments from my brides and their guests. My client Elizabeth Banks chose this style of invitation in celadon green with a contemporary design. The unique presentation has a built-in pocket that's perfect for any inserts, such as your reply card and envelope, direction cards, and weekend itineraries. I closed the invitation with a double wrap of fuchsia waxed twine, accented with complementary beads, which I threaded by hand in the shape of a flower.

It is with joy
and great excitement
that we Invite you to
celebrate the marriage of

JANE
KRUGER

STEPHEN
SCHUSTER

Saturday
At 6 o'clock in the evening
The Seventh of May
2 0 0 5
-
Saint Mary's Cathedral
Mid City Center
-
And afterwards for
cocktails and dinner under the stars
The Mission Observatory
The Rocks, Sydney

Elegant Attire

JACK AND EMILY CONNELLY
TOGETHER WITH SAMUEL AND NANCY STANTON
INVITE YOU TO CELEBRATE THE MARRIAGE OF THEIR CHILDREN

rebecca connelly

&

david stanton

ON SUNDAY AFTERNOON
AT HALF PAST FOUR
07.03.05
~
BY THE GOLDFISH POND
THE CONNELLY ESTATE
EAST HAMPTON
~
COCKTAIL RECEPTION
TO FOLLOW

DRESS SMART

Grace Treson

&

Harrison Wagner

together with their parents
request the honor of your presence
as they begin their life together
as husband and wife

FIVE O'CLOCK ON SATURDAY AFTERNOON
SEPTEMBER TWENTY FOURTH
TWO THOUSAND AND FIVE

THE DESCONSO GARDENS
PASADENA, CALIFORNIA

Celebrations to Continue
Over Cocktails, Dinner and Dancing

Black Tie Optional

Even a simple sheet of card stock can make a lasting impression if you simply play around with wording, font combinations, and layouts. I happen to love square invitations, which are a little twist on the traditional rectangular invitation. These examples offer some wording suggestions.

Three-Dimensional Invitation Variations

◆ For a wedding set in Mexico, guests opened each invitation box to find a miniature bag of corn chips and a tiny jar of salsa with a personalized label with the wedding date. A set of little maracas is a cute alternative (try www.orientaltradingcompany.com for these).

◆ A jar of homemade preserves mailed in a white box was the perfect touch for one bride's wedding, which was being held at her parents' house. As a side benefit, this necessitated a lovely mother-of-the-bride/bride-to-be day of cooking and preserving fresh strawberries. A personalized label with the bride and groom's names, the wedding date, and the location was placed on the front of each jar. The "ingredients" label on the back of each jar listed, in addition to the strawberries, hugs and kisses—a sweet finishing touch. Or, if you aren't up for starting from scratch, repackaging store-bought jelly will work nicely, too.

◆ For one Chinese wedding, I designed little personalized sachets of green tea embossed with the symbol for double happiness. I paired these with a silver tea strainer.

◆ For a wedding that was to take place at a log cabin in upstate New York, an announcement consisted of a tin of hot chocolate and a bag of miniature marshmallows.

◆ Another fun idea is to use a bundle of incense for a Moroccan theme. You can even order unscented incense and dip it in your favorite room spray to create a totally unique fragrance.

wording tips

Incorporating a sense of the setting into the text of the invitation adds a nice personal touch.

◆ At sunset on the island of Jamaica . . .
◆ On the patio . . .
◆ Overlooking the ocean . . .
◆ Poolside at the Bacara Resort . . .
◆ This autumn in the family garden . . .
◆ Under the willow tree . . .
◆ In the northern garden at the El Canto Hotel . . .

Quantity

When adding up your invitation count, remember that a couple requires only one invitation. I recommend ordering about a 10 percent overage on invitations. This will cover any last-minute people joining your guest list, keepsakes, and the fact that at least one or two invitations may get lost in the mail. The mail system is not perfect. I also suggest ordering 20 percent additional envelopes to allow for spelling errors when your invitations are being addressed.

Sealing Your Envelopes

I prefer to seal my envelopes using a permanent glue stick. This prevents any buckling that occurs using the usual "lick and stick" or damp sponge techniques.

REPLY CARDS

A reply or a response card encourages your guests to formally reply to your invitation with an acceptance or a regret. These are most often accompanied by a stamped, pre-addressed envelope. Postcard reply cards are also a fun option. A less formal approach could offer a phone number or an e-mail address to respond to. Typically, the RSVP date is approximately 4 weeks prior to your wedding, though it is always wise to ask your venue when they require a final guest count.

Reply Card Ideas

Instead of the more traditional response choices of "accepts" or "declines," you might also use:

◆ Accepts with pleasure/declines with regret

- Will be there to celebrate/cannot be there to celebrate
- Will be there to celebrate/Will be toasting from afar/Will be with you in spirit

Leaving a blank space after your request for a reply invites guests to be creative in their responses—and the responses themselves make great scrapbook keepsakes. Be sure to number each reply card (delicately in pencil on the back) to correspond to each guest in case someone forgets to write in their name.

Asking guests to enclose a photo of themselves is a great way to collect pictures for later use in personalizing your wedding. You may also like to ask guests to reply with a sentence or two about your relationship. These make wonderful keepsakes.

INSERT CARDS

Insert cards refer to the additional pieces of information you may choose to include in your mailing, such as:

- Direction cards, with or without a map
- Accommodation cards
- Menu cards (if you are asking guests to select an entrée in advance)
- Parking or shuttle information
- A wedding weekend itinerary
- A rehearsal dinner invitation (I often head these with "the night before")
- An invitation to a brunch the following day (which I often introduce with "the morning after")

return address— with a twist

You might want to address your reply card envelopes to one of the following:
- The Bride and Groom to Be
- The Future Mr. and Mrs. Hamilton
- The Parents of the Bride

label your tables

Traditionally, reception tables are numbered. Try writing the number in words or using Roman numerals. Naming your tables is a nice way to personalize. You might like to name your tables after these: artists, cities, colors, currency, drinks/wines, favorite places, flavors of ice cream, flowers/trees, the word "love" in different languages, monuments, movie titles, museums, restaurants, street names, or superheroes.

For a New York wedding, I had table numbers embroidered on cuttings of velvet, which I then cushioned with cotton balls and placed into frames with the glass taken out. These little fabric swatches can later be made into a patchwork keepsake cushion or a baby's quilt, depending on how many tables you have.

You might also like to make tiny art pieces to help guests find their tables. Table numbers on little canvases are very personal, and this is a great time to take advantage of any friends of the family who are artists! Depending on your level of craftiness, you may also like to embark on a detailed art project such as a collage or an oil painting.

◁ The Table and the Twig

Hot glue your table name or number to a branch, which is then inserted into your centerpiece. You can also find some fun posts at craft stores and at floral supply stores if a twig won't suit.

▽ Words on the Wall

For my wedding, I made mosaics of all the table names. We chose places that in chronological order represented the path to our marriage. After the wedding, I strung the mosaics together with leather to make the perfect keepsake for our hallway.

△ Table-Top Twinkle

For an elegant ballroom reception, I stained small wooden plaques (purchased at my local art supply store) and then glued silver Indian paper that I had studded with crystal rhinestones to the front. Each table number, in Roman numerals, was set on a miniature silver easel.

escort cards

Escort cards are the alphabetized list of cards that let your guests know which table they will be sitting at during your reception. Here are some different ways of presenting these.

+ Rows of miniature potted succulents with each guest's name printed on a little herb garden–style label make for a great presentation. They are also a nice little take-home treat for those guests who are not traveling. You could also create a dramatic effect with rows of tall vases displaying a single orchid or a calla lily. Tie guests' names to each vase or secure them in place with a touch of hot glue or double-sided tape.

+ Fill an oversize cylindrical vase lined in garden moss with towering branches of curly willow. Write your guests' names and their table numbers on paper leaves and hang them from the branches as alphabetically as possible. I find this works best when using less than 50 cards; for larger weddings, you may want to do two name card trees.

+ Collect photographs (I love to use baby photos) of all your guests and string these up alphabetically with miniature clothespins. (It helps to have the guests' names on the back with the table number just in case!) You may also like to use pushpins to arrange them artfully onto a giant corkboard. Allow a little time for guests to enjoy looking at all the photos as they search for their own. To collect these photos, ask guests to include a photo of themselves with their reply cards.

pickup sticks

Affix each name card to a stick using permanent glue. Incense sticks or bamboo skewers can work just as well. I have even used coffee stirrers, which you can paint any color you like. Display the sticks in a wooden trough lined with moss and pebbles. Alternatives to a trough could be a wheelbarrow, wooden box, large antique tin washing bucket, small rowboat, or vintage wagon. You may like to line it with wheat grass, sand, or pebbles.

Tip Use sheets of floral foam cut to size to create a base that sticks can be secured to, then cover it with moss or petals.

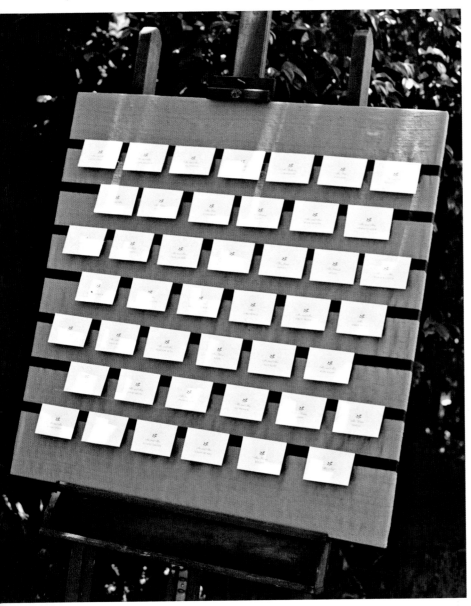

covered in canvas

Display escort cards on a canvas covered in fabric and resting on an easel. (If you're having a large wedding, you may need two.) This is great if space is an issue. My favorite fabric to use is dupioni silk as it has great texture and comes in amazing colors. For this setting, fold your chosen fabric over your canvas and secure using a staple gun. You may need to trim any excess fabric. Plan out the spacing of your escort cards. For example, if you have 80 escort cards, you'll have 8 rows of 10 cards. Add bands of ribbon to secure cards. Slip escort cards or envelopes over the bands of ribbon in alphabetical order.

Tip Using envelopes with guests' names on the front and inserting the printed table name or number is a perfect strategy if you need to shuffle guests' seats at the last minute. You simply remove the guests' old table number and insert the new one—no need to reprint the entire escort card.

under umbrellas

For my wedding, I strung brightly colored cocktail umbrellas attached to each
escort card in the trees lining the entrance to the outdoor dining room. To
do this yourself, tie loose knots in
random intervals along a length of
ribbon, leaving enough length at each
end to tie or nail the ribbon to a tree or
post. Slip the end of each umbrella
through the hole in the knot and tighten.
Attach the cards to the umbrellas by
threading the stick of the umbrella
through hole-punched holes and glueing
to the inside of the card. Hold in place
until the glue dries. Finally, twist each
umbrella so that the guests' names are
facing the same way. Cocktail umbrellas
are available at most party supply stores
or online at www.cocktailumbrellas.com.

place cards

After guests have their escort cards and have made their way to their designated tables, you may then like to assign them a specific place to sit. These place cards are sometimes referred to as name cards or seating cards. Here are some ideas if you choose to use place cards.

+ Write each guest's name in calligraphy on the place card and accent it with crystal rhinestones, pressed flowers, berries, or a fresh flower.

+ Tie place cards to a bundle of incense for a scented treat.

+ Have each guest's name individually printed or written in calligraphy on your menus to kill two birds with one stone!

+ Tie place cards to the stem of each wineglass with a knot of ribbon or bear grass.

+ Have guests' names printed or calligraphed on a band of paper and use this as a napkin ring to fold around each napkin.

+ Write each guest's name on a large river rock—perfect for a garden wedding.

+ For a fall wedding, I had guests' names calligraphed on live autumn leaves and tucked in pocket-folded napkins.

These hand-carved maracas *(left)* were engraved with the bride and groom's names and their wedding date. Place cards were printed on brown paper card stock and tied to the maracas with raffia. These make a sweet take-home memento and are perfect for guests to shake at your grand entrance or at toasts in place of the traditional clapping.

Thread name cards onto twigs and rest alongside each napkin *(bottom, left)*. This looks simple and clean and is great if the wind picks up.

These bold glass bottles *(bottom, middle)* are perfect for adding a punch of color. They cater to windy days, and you can fill them with bath salts, candy, or your favorite olive oil as little favors. I found these at www.orientaltradingcompany.com.

Use baby photographs or a photo of you with the guest to assign seats *(bottom, right)*. This makes for a great personal touch.

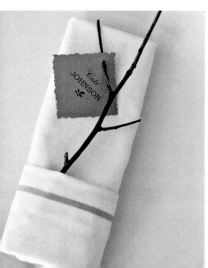

menus

CORRIE & KEN
a wedding celebration

CABO SAN LUCAS . MEXICO . THE 19TH OF FEBRUARY 2005

FIRST COURSE
shrimp cake with
spicy remoulade avocado relish

SECOND COURSE
macadamia crusted sea bass
sautéed vegetables
coconut lime sauce

---

grilled beef tenderloin medallion
wild mushroom crust
madeira wine sauce

DESSERT
soft chocolate "volcano" cake
vanilla ice cream
coconut sauce

Carrie and Peter
A WEDDING FEAST
SANTA BARBARA, CALIFORNIA
THE NINTH DAY OF AUGUST
TWO THOUSAND & THREE

TO START
ICED WATERMELON
AND JICAMA SOUP

SECOND COURSE
YELLOW FIN TUNA CARPACCIO,
PRESSED WITH HEARTS OF PALM,
TANGERINE AND CRACKED PEPPER

ENTREE
PLANTAIN DUSTED GROUPER,
ROASTED RED POTATOES,
CRISPY LEEKS AND A
BERRY MANGO SALSA

OR

PECAN CRUSTED CORNISH HEN
WITH ROAST SUMMER SQUASH
AND SWEET SNAP PEAS
IN A MAPLE GLAZE

DESSERT
ASSORTED BITE SIZED TREATS
CAPPUCCINO AND ESPRESSO
SUMMER BERRIES
WEDDING CAKE

Mr. and Mrs.
James Hamilton
WELCOME YOU TO DINE
NINTH OF JUNE 20...

First Course
MAIN LOBSTER TOWER WITH AVOCADO
GRANNY SMITH APPLES, SWEET CORN AND CITRUS CREAM

Second Course
WHOLE STRIPED BASS FILET WITH ROMA TOMATO
NICOISE OLIVE AND BRAISED FENNEL
OR
GLAZED RACK OF LAMB
TOMATO CONFIT, WHITE BEAN JUS
PENNE WITH ROASTED GARLIC
CAPER AND TOMATO

Dessert
DUO OF CANAPES
CHOCOLATE SAUCE, WILD BERRY COULIS
WEDDING CAKE

Menus can really complement your table
design, especially if your goal is to add a
splash of color. Even if you are not offering
your guests a choice of meals on the day,
it's nice to let your guests know what will be
served. I typically like to design my menus
with a personal heading.

This menu may not be for you, but guests really respond to this nostalgic touch. The headings of "To Start," "Main Course," "Sweet Treats," and "Wedding Cake" flipped open to reveal the menu for each.

I hope my love of stationery has become contagious.

Choosing your invitations can be such a creative and fulfilling part of planning your wedding. Have fun considering all of my stationery ideas, make them your own, and enjoy putting pen to paper, literally!

all dressed up & somewhere to go

It is your wedding day, which means it is your day to shine.

All eyes will be on you, so of course you'll want to look and feel radiant.

Of course, there is no question that there are countless jaw-dropping

couture wedding dresses, and while these gowns don't fit everyone's budget,

they certainly can be wonderful sources of inspiration.

You might opt for a twist on tradition by daring not to wear a dress in a shade of white. I myself walked down the aisle in a dusty rose gown. A dress in shades of ice blue or platinum can also be divine and very flattering. Even adding just a splash of color to a white gown can be striking. Try a satin sash or add straps made of turquoise beads or diamond-like crystals.

I love acting as a stylist to my brides, and after 10 years in the fashion industry, I've found that I have a knack for making fabulous finds in surprising places. I love helping to enhance each woman's personal style, ensuring that she will walk down the aisle glowing with confidence. So now let me pop on my stylist hat and share with you some wonderful ideas on what to wear. But first a little surprise—after all, a bride deserves to be spoiled!

Styling with
monique lhuillier

I have invited star designer Monique Lhuillier to lend her creative genius to the opening pages of this chapter. To me, her gowns epitomize modern bridal luxury and elegance. She has taken the bridal industry by storm with her unique and beautiful designs. For example, she has absolutely perfected the elegant slip gown. Her classic designs would have Cinderella herself shedding tears of joy, and her stylish edginess even has celebrities lining up to wear her gowns.

I am so very honored to have her join me as I present to you a bride's styling fairy tale. For our little experiment, I selected two of Monique's most-requested wedding gowns and styled each of them four different ways. It's amazing the transformation that occurs with just the simplest accessorizing.

earth angel

If your wedding plans include using nature as your backdrop, this style may be perfect for you. Whether your choice of wedding location is a beach setting, a wheat field, a garden, or a forest, embracing earthy elements will enhance your natural glow. Here my bride's loose, windswept curls frame her face. She wears sheer makeup in shades of bronze and a hint of lip gloss. Pearl beaded drop earrings, a shell flower bracelet, and an intricate purse lined in rows of shells are perfect accessories (I found all of these at department stores). And her glass slippers were a pair of leather Roman-style sandals that laced up her calves. Using a Chinese parasol as a prop in formal photographs offers a nice twist.

just a little something

I love to incorporate hair accents. This stunning broach makes a subtle yet striking hair accessory. And if you can't get your hands on real jewels, try your local department stores and boutiques. I actually found this piece at Banana Republic.

Also, a scarf can be the perfect accessory, adding a personal touch in a matter of seconds, which makes for a nice little change for the transition from ceremony to reception. This scarf particularly appealed to me because it had a very Charleston-like feel. You might like to select a scarf in a bright color or even a shawl—or a fur shrug for cooler evenings.

say it in spanish

I love the dramatic feel of this, although obviously, it is not a look everyone would choose! Don't forget that you can keep your look classic for the ceremony itself and then add the somewhat bolder touches such as crimson lips and flowers in your hair for your reception. A low, loose bun is perfect for an accent of fresh flowers. Here I chose burgundy dahlia. In place of a traditional handheld bouquet, I studded a Spanish fan with fresh dahlia. These gold drop earrings are divine and certainly add that Spanish flare. Again, maybe you'd like to wear them for your reception only. I also love the contrast of ruby red nails, but if this is too much of a statement for you, stick with red on your toes.

timeless traditions

This romantic vision was designed around the veil. Here I chose a trailing veil with a slight twist—in place of traditional tulle, this veil is made from a single length of ivory sheer fabric. I accessorized with classic diamonds and a duo of feathers at the V of the bride's neck (these are available through Monique's boutique and can also look great as a hair accessory). I kept the makeup very natural and added some rose-tinged rouge in honor of the quintessential "blushing bride." This classically attired bride wore ivory satin heels and carried an antique pearl clutch I picked up at a vintage store.

cinderella calls

Timeless and classic, this strapless gown epitomizes the fairy tale. Paired with a traditional veil with a blusher (this is the layer of tulle that covers your face on your walk down the aisle) and a bouquet of gardenia surrounded by luscious greens, this bride just takes my breath away. I accessorized with antique jewels and a silver pair of open-toed heels covered in tiny crystals.

marry me modern

Be bold with black and white. A high ponytail wrapped in diamonds and a matching wrist cuff add the perfect edge. The real thing is, of course, wonderful, but a cuff of crystal rhinestones (available at most fabric stores) is a great alternative. Charcoal eye makeup offers a dramatic touch, and a black hand-beaded little cape is the perfect accessory for your reception. And who said brides have to wear white shoes? These divine stiletto strappy sandals are perfect for this modern wedding ceremony, and they are sure to get plenty of wear after the big day, too.

prep in your step

I think this look radiates health and happiness. By adding a pair of red velvet flats and a colorful clutch, you can give a simple dress a whole new feeling. Again, you may prefer to add these accessories at the reception only, keeping a more classic look for the ceremony and then introducing color for the festivities that follow. Replacing a pair of heels with some comfortable flats also pampers a bride's feet!

just a little something

Monique Lhuillier is known for adding sashes to her gowns as a special accessory. You can do the same thing and introduce a touch of color by wrapping a satin sash about your waist. This bride wore classic diamond studs, a bracelet made of jade, and bronze open-toed heels. Her bouquet adds a perfect extra touch of green. I simply wired together assorted succulents to create this unique tropical posy.

The Wedding Dress and

the *magic wand*

The following pages were inspired by my own search for the perfect gown. A designer dress just wasn't in my budget, and so I began to look elsewhere. Along the way, I discovered that sample sales can make all your dreams come true. Most designers have at least two sample sales each year, so if you have your heart set on a Monique Lhuillier gown or a creation from Vera Wang, call their boutiques and inquire about their next sample sale. You may end up getting your dream gown at a fraction of its retail price.

In addition to scouting out local sample sales, I also browsed through countless bridal warehouses—and this is where I discovered that you can get an amazing wedding gown and turn it into a "one-of-a-kind" for much less that you would ever imagine. And so the story begins . . .

Once upon a time, a savvy shopper took a trip to David's Bridal Boutique. She—or should I say I—chose four gowns under $500 each. I consulted bridal magazines and fashion pages (there are amazing gowns in the pages of *Harper's Bazaar*, for example) for some inspiration. I visited fabric stores and craft stores, and then I went to work with a sketch pad and a pencil—aka my magic wand! For under $100 per gown and a little help from my friend with a sewing machine, I brought my ideas to life. (You can always visit your local tailor if sewing is not your forte.) Now each gown looks totally unique, and four very lucky ladies will marry in them and live happily ever after!

cheap tricks

So you've found your dream dress, only it's in the window at Barneys and you're not prepared to blow your entire budget on its price tag. In cases like this, I recommend getting referrals for local dressmakers or tailors and then finding out whether they can inexpensively replicate the dress you have fallen in love with. You'll probably be surprised at the savings, not to mention the fact that you'll be walking down the aisle in a dress made expressly for you!

before

it's a wrap

This elegant strapless gown became a one-of-a-kind original with some creative flourishes. First, I gathered tulle and wrapped it securely around the bride's bodice and across one arm, pinning it in place. Next I carefully transferred the tulle to a 10-inch by 10-inch piece of cardboard that I used as a frame to keep the tulle in place while I beaded. I then hand-sewed beads on the wrapped tulle to mimic the designs already accenting the gown. On the big day, we tied the wrap around the bride, knotted it in the back, and secured it in place using a broach, which allowed the wrap to be easily removed for dancing and rewrapped if desired.

Cost of dress: $499

Cost of alterations: $20 for tulle and beads

Total time: 10 minutes to wrap and 3 hours of hand-beading

after

after

before

strapless

This figure-hugging wedding dress was encrusted with tiny pearl beading. To give the dress a simpler feel, I removed the back straps and then delicately cut off the high neck. I hand-sewed the open seam to create a stunning strapless one-of-a-kind gown.

Cost of dress: $299

Cost of alterations: $3 for thread

Total time: 2 hours to cut and sew and reattach a few fallen pearls

before

gone to waist

This flattering mermaid-style gown was initially accented at the waist with a design created with silver thread and sequins. I added some warmth by covering this accent in a length of latte-colored lace. I hand-sewed the length of lace around the waistline and then cut out little segments to create the peaks at the top and bottom of center. I then sewed on a scattering of tiny freshwater pearls in the middle of random lace flowers as a finishing touch. The neck strap is simply a strand of freshwater pearls attached to the front of the gown and secured using a hook and eye that is hidden in the front of the bodice.

Cost of dress: $349

Cost of alterations: $40 for lace and pearls

Total time: 4 hours to hand-sew lace and pearls

after

after

all laced up

This classic A-line design was transformed into a fairy-tale gown with the help of some antique lace and a few extra hours of work. I removed the satin cuff on the bodice and added an overlay of antique French lace, delicately sewing it in place at the top and around the bust, allowing it to sit freely at the waistline. I also added the lace overlay to the double hem for an additional touch of luxury.

Cost of dress: $349

Cost of alterations: $100 for authentic antique lace (you can buy less expensive lace, but make sure it has a little give to it so it will mold to your body shape)

Total time: 6 hours of sewing

your *glass slipper*

Remember that "bridal" doesn't necessarily mean white. You might choose to step away from the traditional satin pump and look for the perfect pair of silver or bronze wedding shoes. These often look stunning with bridal gowns, and you are much more likely to wear them again afterward. Badgley Mischka, Jimmy Choo, and Manolo Blahnik have stunning shoes to choose from. But if designer shoes aren't for you, the shoes on the opposite page may be exactly what you are looking for.

Tips for Your Toes

Use your wedding shoes as house slippers for a week or two so you can get used to them before your big day. I also recommend having an extra pair of comfortable shoes on standby just in case your other shoes start to hurt your feet. Or, as the evening progresses, treat your tired tootsies to a soft pair of satin ballet slippers, which are available from most dance stores. I order ballet slippers for my brides from www.allaboutdance.com.

A word of caution for all you Dancing Queens: You may fall in love with a pair of slip-ons, but be sure to practice dancing in them—first dance and no ankle strap can be a dangerous combination.

traditions for your toes

* Attaching a penny to the sole of your wedding shoe is said to bring good luck.
* It is a Turkish tradition to have your single girlfriends sign the soles of your wedding shoes (this is perfect to do at your bridal shower). It is said that at the end of your celebration, the girl whose name has faded most will next walk down the aisle.

Stunning Shoes

I went on a little shoe shopping expedition in search of five fabulous finds that I could add my own special flourish to. All of these shoes were less than $100, and with a little imagination and a few extra dollars, I turned them into my own custom creations.

Bronze heels *(far left)*: These simple gold heels become one-of-a-kind originals when you use a hot glue gun to attach tiny pearls to the toe strap of each shoe.

Pink pumps *(second from left)*: A pastel pair of pink leather pointed heels makes a unique wedding accessory when you trim them with cutout designs of antique lace, applied with a hot glue gun.

Silver slip-ons *(middle)*: These friendly flats are accented with dragonfly broaches to add a whimsical sparkle.

Golden flats *(second from right)*: Another pair of comfortably low shoes is made completely unique by adding an intricate gold design, in this case, a pair of costume earrings. I admired the gold filigree detailing, so I removed the earring piece that threads through your ear hole and then hot glued them to the front of these shoes.

Satin stilettos *(far right)*: These platinum satin heels called for a beautiful back. I bought a length of tiny rhinestone rings from my local fabric store, carefully cut them up into individual rings, and pieced them together.

I dyed my own veil a subtle shade of pink to complement my dusty rose gown and sewed clusters of little blush-colored beads all over the comb that secured it.

be jeweled

If it's a cluster of diamonds you envision as the perfect accessory for your bridal gown (but you don't want to spend a lot of money), try visiting your local antique jeweler and inquire about borrowing some jewels for the day. You might also like to wear an heirloom piece to honor your family.

UNVEILING IDEAS

I think a veil completes the picture of what a quintessential bride looks like. The custom of wearing a veil dates back to when lifting your veil represented the handover of the bride from her father's care to her husband's. Today, wearing a veil is more of a personal choice. You may choose to walk down the aisle with your veil back, or you may choose not to wear one at all. Regardless of whether or not you imagine yourself with a veil, I suggest trying one on anyway, just for fun. You may be surprised at what you choose.

You might also want to use craft glue to scatter crystal rhinestones about the length of your veil. This works best if you glue the crystals back to back on either side of your veil. Use pale crystals—otherwise, they could photograph like little black dots.

To add a magical touch, sew delicate pearls along the edge of your veil. Another option is to find out if your mother or grandmother has saved her wedding veil. If so, it would be touching to carry on a family tradition.

THE PERFECT PURSE

Scouring vintage stores often produces some wonderful finds, and at wonderful prices, too!

Accent your clutch by studding it with fresh flowers using a hot glue gun. I like to use orchids and dahlias, since they tend to be the more resilient blooms. I find that colored flowers tend to last longer as white petals tend to bruise and discolor easily.

A Peek in Your Purse

In addition to being a lovely accessory, your purse is the perfect place to tuck away a few important items you might need during the course of your big day.

+ A pint-size packet of moist towelettes or wipes can come in very handy, whether to clean your feet after a beach ceremony, to spot out a little makeup stain on your dress, or just to refresh throughout the evening.

+ Tissues for those tears of joy are a must.

+ With all those congratulatory hugs and kisses, make sure you have fresh breath. I'd shy away from gum in case it shows in your photographs, but do opt for mints!

This velvet purse is brought to life with just a single burgundy dahlia. I affixed it with a hot glue gun before the wedding.

something blue

+ Have your husband-to-be's name embroidered in blue on your underwear—something a little sweet and just a little bit naughty!

+ Glue a tiny blue rhinestone to your lingerie.

+ Sew a small sapphire or aquamarine pendant onto your undergarment or add it to your bouquet.

+ A blue garter is the traditional way to go!

bridal kit 911

Along with a backup of wipes, tissues, and mints, here's what I always have on hand for my brides.

+ A miniature sewing kit, available at most drugstores
+ Safety pins
+ Hair pins and bands
+ Tampons
+ Pain relievers
+ Deodorant
+ Nail file
+ Adhesive bandages
+ Double-sided tape (for wayward hemlines)
+ Crazy glue
+ Pen
+ A backup contact sheet with all the vendors' details—just in case

Finally, having your checkbook and a little cash handy can be a lifesaver for any last-minute bills or tips.

DRESSING YOUR BRIDESMAIDS

There is no rule of thumb about how many bridesmaids to have in your wedding party. This decision is entirely yours to make. And don't feel obligated to have equal numbers of bridesmaids and groomsmen. Of course, it looks more symmetrical when there are equal numbers, but it is not necessary.

Bridesmaids these days aren't bound to the old-fashioned tradition of all wearing the same dress in the same fabric. Lots of brides love mixing it up. You may like to have all of the girls wear the same dress in different colors or wear different dresses but in the same fabric. The latter is a perfect way to accommodate the different body shapes of your maids. After all, it's important for your bridesmaids to feel comfortable, too, and this way each can choose a style that complements her individual figure.

These simple, elegant dresses were designed by Saeyoung at Saeyoung Vu Couture (VuCouture.com). We chose three shades of dupioni silk to create three different, simple yet elegant dresses that your maids would die to wear.

A "bridesmaid dress" doesn't necessarily have to be "bridal." I have found some amazing dresses at regular boutiques and department stores, dresses that will definitely be worn again after the wedding is just a beautiful memory. I found these great dresses at the store Anthropologie.

wedding day warmth

After your ceremony and as the sun sets, you may like to take off your veil and pop on a little shawl for warmth as well as variety. This blush pink feathered shrug *(top)* gives this classy bride a whole new look. For a winter wedding, a cashmere poncho can be a stunning accessory. A fitted white coat or a delicate fur cape could also perfectly complement your dress—and you can always wear it again with a pair of jeans.

For those cooler months or for later in the evening, offer guests (just account for the ladies, as men most often have a jacket) pashminas to keep them warm. I buy mine downtown in the fabric district for $6 each! Display them in a wooden box with a label such as "Please take a shawl and snuggle" or "Perfect for a chilly evening." They look great rolled or stacked in neatly folded piles. These also make sweet take-home gifts.

FLOWER GIRLS

I'm pretty sure almost every little girl loves to dress up in tulle. These fuchsia pink flower girl dresses, inspired by ballet tutus, were made by Saeyoung at Saeyoung Vu Couture. As with bridesmaids' dresses, don't feel like you need to buy standard flower girl dresses either. An off-the-rack party dress can also be adorable and can be worn again to a birthday party or some other event.

- ✦ Adding a delicate pair of fairy wings provides a touch of magic and can be perfect for an outdoor ceremony.

- ✦ Feathered butterflies look so sweet in the hair of your little ones.

- ✦ Applying a little body glitter (aka fairy dust) can be a lifesaver for any lurking temper tantrums, and it adds a beautiful shimmer, too.

- ✦ Your flower girls are sure to love a pair of ballet slippers topped with butterflies. I found these feather butterflies (*bottom*) at my local craft store and affixed them using hot glue. Alternatively, accents of crystal rhinestones add a sweet sparkle.

From head to toe, you deserve to feel like a princess. Enjoy your search for the perfect gown. Try on as many styles as you need to. Bring family or friends to save you from indecisiveness, and don't forget to venture into every store with an open mind. I have found amazing accessories in such stores as Banana Republic—I'm sure they weren't designed for brides, but it doesn't matter.

Take advantage of the smorgasbord available to you as a consumer. Make it a real event. Happy shopping!

blissful blooms

Flowers just happen to be **my favorite element** of event planning.

There is something quite magical about working with

such perfections of nature. And coincidentally my path

into wedding coordination was literally paved with roses.

It all started when my girlfriend, a bride-to-be, received an outrageous quote

for her wedding flowers. I said to myself, "I think I can do that"—

and so I did! I ventured down to the flower markets, I experimented,

and I researched, always adding my own style.

My friend's wedding flowers turned out to be the talking point of her reception—and we saved her a pretty penny in the process. After all, as beautiful as flowers can be, they don't have to consume your entire budget. So let's slip on some comfortable shoes and tiptoe through those tulips, so to speak!

CONSIDER YOUR CHOICES

Nature has blessed us with so many captivating flower varieties, but you can't have them all—you have to choose. But before deciding on your blooms, you may need to backtrack a little and focus on the overall vision for your wedding. I recommend starting a scrapbook with magazine clippings of and references to flowers and everything else that you are drawn to. It makes a great keepsake, and it will come in very handy for your trip to the floral designer and your other vendors. Let's face it, unless you're a florist or an avid gardener, you probably don't know the names of all the flowers that have captured your attention. Consider these helpful hints when making flower decisions.

+ Choosing flowers that are in season will lower your flower quote. In-season flowers also tend to be the freshest. Check with a local florist on what is available at the time of your wedding. There is no point in wishing for peonies in February—even if you could find them, they would cost a fortune—though you can always splurge on them for your bouquet.

+ If you are trying to save a little money on the cost of your flowers, here's a tip: Avoid planning your wedding for just before Mother's Day or Valentine's Day, when flowers are much more expensive.

+ When contemplating flowers, consider the weather. For example, gardenias in the sweltering heat will wilt and discolor very quickly. Orchids, on the other hand, are far more resilient.

◆ Another suggestion: If you or your friends are going to do your flowers instead of going with a florist or planner, opt for long-lasting blooms so you can work with them a day or two before, so you don't have to add this to your list of worries on the day of your wedding. In addition, I always advise doing up one sample of your flower arrangements first, just to be sure you are happy with the way they look. You may even wish to take a picture of the sample so you can use it as your template later.

BLOOMS FOR THE BRIDE

Your bouquet should first of all make you smile, since it will have the honor of accompanying you down the aisle to marriage. There are so many bouquet choices available. I recommend flipping through bridal magazines to better grasp the variety. You should also consider the shape of your dress when choosing your bouquet: For example, a simple slip dress might look better with a decadent cluster of flowers, while a fuller gown might look better with a smaller posy.

I personally love color for a bouquet—it's fun and it's festive. I love the contrast with white and the way color translates in photographs. That's not to say that an armful of white orchids doesn't impress me! It's just that I think of a white bouquet as more traditional, and this is where I like to add a little twist!

Let's take a peek at some of my most-talked-about bouquets . . .

sweet touches for your bouquet

◆ Consider sprinkling fine glitter dust over your bouquet just prior to your ceremony to highlight the fairy-tale moment.

◆ A light coating of floral spray over your bouquet adds a dewy feel (this is really only appropriate for sturdy blooms and not delicate flowers such as gardenias).

◆ For the cover of *InStyle Weddings*, I added fresh sprigs of mint to Megan Mullally's bouquet. Lavender and rosemary also emit a wonderful natural fragrance.

◆ Pop an ornamental butterfly or a ladybug (for good luck) on your bouquet. Inserting a scattering of wired pearls throughout your bouquet is a lovely subtle touch.

Taken with Tulips
This classic spring bouquet of striped tulips was tied with a band of hot pink satin ribbon. I incorporated highlights of the couple's love story by printing them on a strip of pale pink card stock and hot-gluing it to the base. If you have kept love letters from your courtship, you may like to attach these to your bouquet instead. Writing out your personal vows is another idea.

◁ Green with Envy

This tropical cluster is filled with berzilla berries, miniature pineapple stems, and flowers hand woven from palm fronds. Wrapped with aspidistra leaves at the base, this unique bouquet is one of my favorites.

▽ Orchids on Your Arm

This bouquet has a special place in my heart. It is actually what I carried down the aisle, only mine was in shades of dark pink. Here these citrus-toned cymbidium orchids are cradled by a banana leaf and tied with lily grass.

△ The Bold and the Beautiful

A cluster of black calla lilies makes a striking bouquet, and it's quite easy to make yourself. Secure the lilies with a band of green floral tape and then wrap them in a cuff of diamond crystals. An *In-Style* story with Leslie Bibb featured this bouquet of lilies tied with a strand of carrie shells. A silver cuff is a great alternative.

▽ Flowers for Fall

A fall wedding in a wheat field inspired this earthy bouquet. Together with dried artichokes and handfuls of wheat thistles, these dried flowers are perfect for an autumn walk down the aisle. I secured the base with a wide band of chocolate brown woven straw that I found at my local fabric store.

△ Poppies Please

This loose gathering of vibrant poppies tied with string radiates happiness. Casual and carefree, these hand-picked blooms offer such a fresh burst of color.

▷ Broach the Subject

This mix of full-bloomed tangerine roses is surrounded by ruscus leaves and accented with two lengths of contrasting ribbon. I used a broach of diamond flowers to secure the ribbon—if you have one as a family heirloom, this makes a great personal touch.

70

Perfect Peonies

Fit for a queen, these decadent burgundy double-faced peonies were held by Molly Shannon as she walked down the aisle. I designed this bouquet in memory of Molly's parents. I secretly collected old photographs of her mother and father, reduced them on a photocopier, affixed them to card stock (both back and front), and tied them onto her bouquet with delicate strands of ribbon. This way, when she walked down the aisle, both of her parents accompanied her.

floral accessories

Have your florist wire some
fresh blooms to place in your
hair. Even if you are wearing a
veil, you may want to remove it
for your reception, in which
case a full-bloomed rose or
king-size orchid secured behind
one ear could look ravishing!
Wiring flowers as bracelets and
anklets is also a sweet idea at
the right wedding.

BLOOMS FOR YOUR BRIDESMAIDS

It is nice if your maids' flowers complement yours; here are a few ideas to get you started.

+ Have your maids carry smaller versions of your bouquet.

+ Have each maid carry a posy of different flowers, but in the same shade. One friend could carry terra-cotta roses, another rust-colored orchids, another burnt orange tulips, for example.

+ Using the same flowers but tying them with different but complementary ribbon or fabric often looks great.

+ Personalize each bouquet by accenting it with a gift. Attaching a broach or an item of jewelry is perfect.

+ Flowers for your maids' hair might be a nice idea. My two bridesmaids each wore a delicate butterfly in her hair.

FLOWERS FOR YOUR OTHER SPECIAL LADIES

It might be nice to give your mothers a corsage or a floral bracelet or even a bouquet of their own. Try to coordinate their flowers with the colors of their outfits. You might like to attach a scrolled note letting them know how much you appreciate the way they have touched your life. Consider ordering personal flowers for grandparents and stepparents, too.

flowers for the *little ones*

These "princess hats" *(top)* are perfect for housing flower girl petals. I hot-glued a variety of lengths of doubled-faced satin ribbon to paper party hats, slightly overlapping each length of ribbon over the last. The variety of ribbons available allows you to coordinate these flower girl treats perfectly with the colors of your wedding.

A ring of orchids *(bottom)* to carry down the aisle is sure to make any girl smile. You may also use this as a crown. Alternatively, a ring of butterflies looks sweet, and this is perfect for venues that don't permit petals to be sprinkled down the aisle.

A fairy-tale or garden setting might be perfect for your flower girls to carry a miniature birdcage filled with ivy vines and night jasmine.

boutonnieres
for the *Men*

When deciding on your boutonnieres, remember that there will be many congratulatory hugs taking place. Choose a resilient bloom, as delicate flowers mean you may need a handful of refresher boutonnieres on standby.

+ This boutonniere *(top)* is a little less traditional. These berries are from the eucalyptus family and have been wrapped in strips of aspidistra leaves.

+ I adore orchids. This simple but striking boutonniere *(bottom)* is a single phalaenopsis orchid backed with a pair of lemon leaves and three loops of lily grass.

+ For a fall wedding, I designed a boutonniere with a miniature pinecone backed by ruscus leaves.

+ Snowberries can make an impressive boutonniere.

+ For a wedding at an old Hollywood mansion, the groom's boutonniere was a single white calla lilly backed with a stunning peacock feather.

FLOWERS FOR THE RECEPTION

The flowers that grace your dining tables can light up a room. Take a moment to picture yourself walking into your wedding reception. Is there something specific that you see on the center of your tables? You may have something clean and simple in mind, or maybe you are imagining a tower of roses to impress. Either way, you may like to consider these tips.

+ Make sure guests can see each other from across the table. Ideally, centerpieces should be tall and skinny or short and fat! I like to set a sample table for my clients. This way, they can formally approve their dining experience well before their big day.

+ There is no rule insisting on having the same centerpieces at each table, although you may like to design in the same color palette using a variety of blooms. For example, try white ranunculus at some tables, white roses at others, and white peonies at the rest. If you are setting a banquet table, consider smaller versions of the main centerpieces to run down the middle of the table. You may also want to vary centerpieces by height, alternating between tall and short. And if you have differently shaped tables (I love to mix long tables with square and round), then you may like to choose a different but complementary flower arrangement for each table shape.

+ Don't be afraid to ask your florist if you can buy your own vases if they don't have the perfect one to offer. I've found amazing and affordable vases at stores such as Ikea and Cost Plus and at www.westelm.com.

+ Maybe you are considering flowerless centerpieces. Candles can make a grand statement. Be careful to account for the wind if you are dining outdoors. Lemon and lime pyramid centerpieces have wowed many guests. Assorted sizes of wooden pails of peaches, plums, and nectarines can make a perfect autumn centerpiece. A vase filled with giant ivory feathers and white peonies graced the tables at a Charleston-inspired wedding.

+ Plants can make beautiful centerpieces—I've placed rows of spring daffodils potted in moss pots down a banquet table. A Santa Barbara wedding was dressed with maiden ferns in woven leather boxes packed with moss. Succulents come in amazing varieties also.

vivacious vessels

It's amazing the difference the vase can make. Glass vases can look amazing. The glass vases on the opposite page are lined in four different ways.

Don't feel confined to a traditional glass vase, though. I have designed centerpieces in an assortment of containers, such as the following:

+ Chocolate brown glass vases were home to dozens of pale pink orchids and chocolate cosmos.

+ Modern wooden boxes have overflowed with hand-opened striped roses. (They are called 'Intuition'.)

+ Watering cans (for a rustic effect, oxidize them using antiquing fluid available at the hardware store) are sweet for a garden gathering as are hand-painted buckets or assorted sizes of glass jars wrapped in bear grass.

+ A cluster of Moroccan tea glasses scattered about the center of a table can create the perfect ambience in the right setting.

+ Cover a wooden box in fabric using a staple gun, or cover the box in clumps of moss using hot glue for a great earthy texture.

This arrangement of simple dogwood branches *(left)* was presented in a cylindrical vase with a base of white pebbles.

Line your vase with horsetail bamboo. This bathroom arrangement of lime green cymbidium orchids *(bottom, left)* is the perfect complement.

Use stephanotis flowers to surround your vase. I also like to line glass vases in rose petals. Try to face the velvet side of the petal toward the glass. This centerpiece *(bottom, middle)* has a handful of calla lilies tied with a knot of bear grass in the center and a mix of greens and hypericum berries surrounding them.

This spring centerpiece *(bottom, right)* was lined with assorted tropical leaves. I love to use aspidistra leaves, galex leaves, and striped ti leaves.

Light My Fire

Lighting is key during an evening celebration. Candles are a must, assuming fire permits allow. In lieu of a more traditional floral centerpiece, these tables were home to Moroccan lanterns surrounded by red rose petals. If petals are being placed directly on dining tables, I like to use the petals from fresh roses, de-petaled on the spot, instead of scattering prepackaged petals. This way, you avoid any soggy or discolored petals appearing right in your guests' eye line.

◁ All about Bamboo

I seem to be drawn to Asian elements. These fuchsia pink mokara orchids graced the square tables at my own Balinese-inspired wedding reception. I made these vessels from cuttings of bamboo. I bought bamboo poles from my local hardware store and had them cut into varying heights. I crazy-glued them in groups of nine and lined them with plastic to create one-of-a-kind vases.

▽ Wishing for Willow

I think curly willow has a very storybook feel to it. These tables were centered around a wooden box lined with mood moss and glazed black pebbles. Each box featured the tips of curly willow branches scattered with white wired cymbidium orchids. The trick is to not overfill the box with willow so that guests can easily see those sitting across from them.

△ Garden Glory

Setting long tables is my favorite. It kind of reminds me of royalty, I guess. I accented this table set for 12 with a sage green burlap table runner and assorted moss ceramic pots filled with a variety of greens. I chose garden mint, rosemary (because I love the smell), cabbage flowers, potted green hydrangea, ruscus accented with hypericum berries, and artichoke stems.

FLOWERS FOR YOUR COCKTAIL HOUR

Since the cocktail hour is typically the introduction to the wedding reception, I like to keep the floral design consistent between the two. This doesn't mean duplicating your centerpieces; it simply means that it is nice to keep everything complementary. This may be accomplished via the style of flowers—all modern versus all traditional—or by the color: red amaryllis for the cocktails and red roses for the reception, for example. Here are some flowers that often make appearances at my clients' cocktail hours.

Arrangements. Set up a few cocktail tables in the cocktail area. These may be stand-up tables or sit-down tables with chairs (offering some seating is nice, especially for elderly guests) or both and are traditionally covered in linens. If you are planning on a lounge room setup, you might want to place flowers on the coffee tables, too. Consider these five simple favorites.

+ A shallow bowl lined with river rocks and filled with floating dahlia or gardenia blooms

+ Cylindrical vases filled with water and submerged cymbidium orchids create a wonderful magnifying effect.

+ Giant elephant palms in giant cylindrical vases filled with water

+ Potted cacti flowers (succulents) displayed in moss-lined silver metal boxes or glass vases lined in moss. Or perhaps potted orchids or herbs are more suited to your celebration.

+ A beautiful vase with a narrow neck displaying a single flower. I have found perfect ones at stores such as Crate and Barrel, or you may like to splurge and buy more of an art piece to keep for your home. These vases also make great gifts afterward—maybe one each for your bridesmaids?

Bars. It's nice to accent your bars. Just make sure there will be enough room for your server to tend to guests first. You will also want to choose an arrangement that is quite sturdy and not easy to knock over. Try large hurricane vases filled with kumquats, pomegranates, fresh cranberries, or lemons and limes (a few cross sections here look great). You may also want to add some towering curly willow branches or blossom branches.

Cocktails. Fresh orchid skewers can add a beautiful touch of color to your cocktails. Be sure to have your caterer wash them thoroughly beforehand.

Hors d'oeuvres. Use leaves and fresh flowers to decorate trays for the cocktail hors d'oeuvres. Again, be sure to wash them thoroughly first.

ACCENT FLOWERS

It's often the little things that make a big difference. Look at your venue with the less obvious areas in mind. Maybe there's a great statue that you can add a flower to, or an easel that you can cover with garden ivy, or a fireplace or a fountain . . .

Fireplace. Line a fireplace mantle with tall vases filled with dendrobium orchids or calla lilies, for example. And if it's a working fireplace and not 100 degrees outside, make sure there are plenty of logs. If it is a nonworking fireplace, inquire as to whether a cluster of various sizes of pillar candles is permitted.

Fountain. If your location has a fountain, float flowers in the water. You may also like to set up a little wishing area with a box of pennies and a sign inviting your guests to make a wish and toss a penny into the fountain. Dahlias and gardenias are great floating flowers.

Pool. Try floating candles or flowers in the pool if your location has one. Remember that filters tend to draw floating items to one section of the pool, so you may want to weigh things down using string and little weights.

Restrooms. Blooms in the bathrooms make a nice impression. If you don't want an elaborate arrangement for this room, try a potted orchid instead. You may also like to use your favorite scented candle. Votivo's red currant scent is very popular. Placing river rocks on the hand basins is a great, easy, and affordable touch. Rose petals lining the basins can also look lovely. Be sure to check first that they can't get caught and clog the drain. And if your guests will be washing their hands with hot water, you may want to reconsider using petals in favor of pebbles, as petals will wilt as the night progresses. In the men's room, I always place petals in a urinal—it can be quite a talking point, trust me. Men don't tend to notice many of the details, but they certainly will remember this one!

Flowers can really set the tone for your celebration, so let choosing them

be something you have fun with. Spend time considering your options

and visiting the varieties of blooms available. A trip down to your local flower market may

just become your favorite morning pastime . . . just look at what happened to me!

to love and honor

Ultimately, **the most important thing** about your big day is that it is a fabulous celebration of **your union of love.** The ceremony is your opportunity to **share this love** with your family and friends.

Whether you treat guests to an exchange of your most personal vows or have them wave tangerine streamers as you walk back down the aisle after the ceremony is complete, your wedding day provides the perfect chance to let your love story shine.

I have tied little tags to bottles with notes such as "Cheers, Max and Jen" or "Enjoy," along with the date.

WONDERFUL WELCOMES

Offering guests a little something on arrival is a thoughtful touch. Consider welcoming your family and friends with one of the following special treats.

◆ An old-fashioned lemonade stand is the perfect way to greet guests as they arrive for an outdoor ceremony. Serve traditional lemonade or add a twist and serve mint or watermelon lemonade, basil cucumber water, or chilled green infused tea, for example.

◆ Little bottles of chilled seltzer (I love lemonatas and Perrier water, too) are always popular. If you don't have waitstaff to butler-pass these, line the chilled bottles up on a table or keep them on ice so guests can help themselves.

◆ At some winter weddings, I have served arriving guests hot chocolate or hot apple cider (spiked and unspiked) in mismatched china teacups or oversize coffee mugs as a sweet welcome treat.

◆ Butler-passed cocktails served on arrival also make a great first impression. You might decide on a signature cocktail (an apple martini, for example), champagne garnished with fresh berries or a splash of peach nectar, or a nonalcoholic freshly squeezed juice.

◆ At my wedding, I asked a girlfriend to hand out little wired feather butterflies to each of the ladies as they arrived. They then pro-

Offer Chinese parasols to help shade the sunshine at an outdoor wedding. A note such as "Please shade yourself" is a nice touch.

ceeded to pop them into their hair, attach them to their purses, or tie them around their wrists. It was so much fun catching a glimpse of everyone still wearing them throughout the evening. A fresh flower for each guest is another alternative. I love to use wired orchids: The women can wear them as hair accessories, and the men can enjoy them as boutonnieres.

MUSIC

Fill the air with music as guests are arriving. Dare to move away from the traditional string quartet and consider something a little different. A mariachi or a flamenco band might be the perfect way to start your celebration. A sitar player or a trio of Jamaican-style drummers could also be cool depending on the style of your wedding.

love letters

Write each other a little note that you can each open separately before you walk down the aisle (make sure there is enough time to attend to your makeup after probable tears of joy!). You may also like to give each other a gift. This gift may be as decadent as diamonds or as sweet as a hand-written promise from the groom to get rid of his favorite pair of cowboy boots after years of his bride's pleading.

Here are eight great songs to walk down the aisle to. Some are classics and some are a little offbeat and unexpected.

1. "Every Morning"—Keb' Mo'
2. "Blower's Daughter"—Damien Rice
3. "Feels like Home"—Randy Newman
4. "Somewhere over the Rainbow"—Israel Kamakawiwo'ole
5. "Take My Breath Away"—Tuck and Patti
6. "For You"—Duncan Sheik
7. "Northern Sky"—Nick Drake
8. "Love Me Tender"—Norah Jones

Music Notes

Music is such a personal choice. I like to capture each couple's personality within the songs that make up the sound track to their wedding. Here are some suggestions to help the process go smoothly.

- In the months leading up to your wedding, keep a little notebook with you so that you can jot down tunes you overhear on the radio or while you're out that would be great for your wedding day. This way, you won't forget them when it's time to select your music.

- A marriage ceremony rarely runs perfectly on schedule, so remember to account for a late start when booking your musicians and have an overtime rate agreed upon in writing beforehand.

- Once you've hired musicians for your ceremony, take advantage of their experience and ask them for song suggestions.

- Before determining the volume of your music, take into account the number of guests and your location. Outdoor weddings often require amplification, whereas an indoor wedding provides insulation and amplification may not be necessary.

- When deciding where to position musicians, look at the site from the photographer's point of view. You probably don't want a string quartet to be the highlight of all your photos, so you might opt to position them on the periphery.

- If you're having an outdoor wedding, remember that wood instruments often cannot be in direct sun. Find a shaded area or set up an umbrella overhead for your musicians.

- Give your musicians a list of your processional and recessional, noting who walks down to what song.

- Ask your music company or musicians to compile a CD for you of all the songs they played at your wedding. It makes a great keepsake.
- In lieu of live music for your ceremony, consider having your DJ play selected tunes.

TAKE YOUR SEATS

Try to be creative with your seating plan. Setting up your chairs in a semi-circle can make for a more intimate ceremony. Or you might even like to opt for a full circle. If your ceremony location allows chairs to be arranged in the round, remember to leave little access aisles so guests can get to their seats easily. I also like the symbolism of being married inside a circle of your family and friends.

Instead of using traditional folding chairs or chiavari chairs, look into renting (or even buying) something a little different to enhance the feel of your ceremony. Here are some alternative choices I've used.

- Comfortable couches, modern or eclectic
- Bamboo chairs
- Park benches
- Little square ottomans
- Oversize cushions
- Deck chairs (these look amazing lined up at a beach ceremony)
- Picnic rugs for a casual, intimate exchange

Ikea has some great affordable chairs. If you're worried about your budget, depending on the style and quantity of chairs you're thinking about purchasing, you might want to check with a few local rental companies to see if they are interested in buying them from you after the wedding.

You can dress up chairs by using seat covers. I sometimes like to accessorize further by tucking stems of dendrobium orchids in the slipcover tie. Chiavari chairs or bamboo folding chairs interlaced with threaded orchids, ivy, or smilax also look amazing.

something for *each seat*

programs

Programs typically describe how your ceremony will unfold and list your immediate families and the names of those who will walk down the aisle before you. Notes about music and readings are commonly included as well. A program is also the perfect place to cite loved ones who cannot be there to share in your day, or you may thank your guests for traveling to be with you or your families for hosting your celebration.

Make your guests feel special by placing a little something at each ceremony chair. Here are a handful of my favorites.

+ To create a real party atmosphere, place streamers and whistles on each chair to celebrate after you are pronounced husband and wife.

+ I worked with one couple where the bride was French and the groom American, so they had their guests wave their respective country's flags as they walked back down the aisle as man and wife. These flags greeted guests as they took their seats and had a tag that read "Please wave after the kiss."

+ For an evening ceremony, having guests hold lit sparklers can look amazing as you leave the altar. Place sparklers and matches on each ceremony seat with a note to ignite at "the kiss." Or use sparklers in place of a champagne toast at the reception. I always love having guests wave them as the bride and groom say farewell. (Don't forget to be sure that sparklers are legal in your state!)

+ Some couples love to have their guests blow congratulatory bubbles after their ceremony (my theory is that it reminds them of their childhoods!).

+ One of my brides was a flight attendant, so I placed little paper airplanes on each chair and guests launched them into flight when the bride and groom kissed. They were old school–style planes I had had preprinted with the instruction: "Please set into flight at the kiss." The photos of the wedding "launch" were fabulous. You don't have to work as a flight attendant to enjoy this sweet touch!

The fan program reads:

MEGAN & STEVE
cabo san lucas · mexico
02 · 19 · 05

PARENTS OF THE BRIDE
michael & janie cross

MAID OF HONOR
tamara peters

BRIDESMAIDS
jennifer adams
penny barrows

PARENTS OF THE GROOM
jill mitchell & ken bilks

BEST MAN
michael cross

GROOMSMEN
stephen fuller
jason middleton

CELEBRANT
judge christopher stone
· · ·
WEDDING WELCOME
PERSONAL VOWS
BLESSINGS
WINE CEREMONY
EXCHANGE OF RINGS
READING
"i carry your heart within me" by e.e. cummings
read by helen burrington
PRAYERS
KISSING OF THE BRIDE!
· · ·
thank you for celebrating with us.
to our parents, we thank you from the bottom of our hearts
for your love, support, and wonderful memories.

▽ Fan Fair

Sandalwood fans with personalized labels or studded with fresh flowers are sweet and perfect for a summer's day. These fans were personalized with little hangtags from www.myownlabels.com.

△ A Perfect Program

My favorite program offers a little breeze on a summer's day and doubles as a favor for your guests to take home. I found these silk-screen fans in L.A.'s Chinatown. The program information is printed on heavy card stock, custom cut, and then affixed to the back of each fan using all-purpose craft glue.

▷ Confetti Please

Tossing confetti petals makes for great photo opportunities on your walk back down the aisle. These triangular pouches from Pantry Press (www.pantry-press.net) are perfect for holding a couple of handfuls. Be sure to tie the ribbon loosely enough for guests to be able to get the petals out!

aisle runners

Church Chic

A church will often speak for itself in terms of style. A simple scattering of petals, altar arrangements, and fragrant Casablanca lilies at the ends of each pew can really add an element of style. Many churches have strict rules about flowers and candles. Check with the event manager first.

◁ Fun with Fabric

For Fred Savage's wedding to Jennifer Stone, I used a roll of upholstery fabric to create a unique aisle runner. I had their ceremony tent draped in sage green sheer fabric and hung a giant Chinese lantern covered in fresh orchids from each peak of the tent. Before guests arrived, I strolled through the tent spraying Votivo's red currant room spray to offer a scented welcome.

▽ A Woven Walk

This ceremony took place under a modern custom-made gazebo that was laced with a waterfall of wired dendrobium orchids. The chocolate brown woven straw aisleway was scattered with orchids, and guests kept cool with fans also accented with fresh orchids that I'd attached with hot glue that morning.

△ Blinded by Love

At my wedding, I walked down an aisle I had decorated by joining together bamboo blinds. After removing the blind strings and metal parts, I linked them together using twine, and then secured them directly to the lawn using tent pegs. A sea of petals or orchid blooms scattered down your aisle can make a grand statement.

You might like to line your aisleway with one of the following:

- For a romantic mood, use pillar candles in oversize cylindrical vases. You might like to line them with rose petals, orchids, sand, or baby pinecones, for example.
- Opt for stand-up lanterns. (I often rent them from a local Moroccan store.)
- Giant pinwheels look great lining a breezy, sandy aisle.
- Tiki torches (if the wind permits) are easy and fun.
- Strands of pearls or lush garlands can look sweet strung from chair to chair. Note that guests will have to enter and take their seats from the outside of the rows, as the aisle-side entrance will be blocked.

UNDER AN ARCH

Don't feel that you need to overwhelm an arch or an arbor in an abundance of blooms. Sometimes simpler is better. You should be the center of attention during your ceremony, not your flowers. If you opt for an arbor, you might try using fabrics or vines as an accent.

Take advantage of any friends or family who have a knack for carpentry. At one of my weddings, for example, the bride's father built a wooden arch that to this day remains in her backyard and is now covered with night-blooming jasmine. (*A little tip:* You can always rent an arch from your florist or buy one directly from a gardening store.)

If you'd like, you can have your guests decorate your arch for you. Offer guests a flower as they make their way to your ceremony site. Before they take their seats, have each guest tuck their flowers into your arch with a wish. (It helps if the arch has vines or greenery added beforehand so that the flowers can be inserted easily.) Just think: You will be wed under an arch blessed with wonderful wishes from your family and friends.

Covered by a Chuppah

If you are having a Jewish ceremony and will be married beneath a chuppah, ask if there is an heirloom tallit in the family. You may like to substitute a tallit for a family quilt or a tablecloth, providing it is appropriate for your style of ceremony. For one bride, I had a tallit created using fabric from her mother's wedding dress. Alternatively, drape an heirloom veil over the top of your chuppah. I always love using amazing fabrics overhead. You may also like to personalize your tallit or overhead fabric by having it embroidered with something special to you, such as traditional scripture or a monogram. After your ceremony, you can use this fabric to make keepsake cushions for your home.

ALL THAT WORDS CAN SAY

ceremony bound

Whether you will be married in a church by a priest or under a chuppah by a rabbi, you may need to follow the format of a traditional religious ceremony. However, if you are permitted to take liberties with the ceremony, here are some of my favorite ideas.

Instead of having the person officiating your wedding read from a handful of loose pages, write out (or print out and paste) your ceremony in a beautiful journal. This makes a great keepsake, too. There are some magnificent leather-bound journals available and some gorgeous fabric-covered ones, too. Try Urban Outfitters or The Art Store for something cool and affordable.

+ Include the story of how you met in your ceremony. It allows your guests to experience part of your love story. In place of a more formal reading, my husband and I asked a friend to highlight the humor of our courtship and tell the story of how we got together.

+ Remember that exchanging wedding vows is really the heart of the entire celebration. If you can muster up the courage, reading your own specially written vows to one another not only makes for a special treat for your guests but will also give you and your husband an unforgettable memory to forever look back on.

+ During one of my all-time favorite ceremonies, the bride and groom read aloud from a series of love letters they had written to each other when they first started dating.

+ Friends of mine structured their vows by listing all the reasons they fell in love with each other ("I love you because . . . "), then all the things they were thankful for, and finally all the promises they wanted to make to each other. They included silly, funny moments as well as all the tear-jerking commitments. I loved it so much I wrote my own vows in a similar way.

Just in case you are looking for help creating your ceremony, I offer you a peek at mine. I was married by Robert A. Ringler of Bel-Air Wedding Ceremonies. My husband and I worked with him to put together a ceremony unique to us. But feel free to borrow from this in whatever way you want.

my ceremony

Introduction

Would everybody please rise.

(Bride enters.)

You may now be seated.

Good afternoon and a special welcome. It is my great pleasure to begin tonight's celebrations as Christopher Russell Gartin and Joanne Catherine Ahlfeld will join together to become Mr. and Mrs. Christopher Gartin.

Thank you to everyone who spent many patient hours traveling to be here with us. Your presence is a true testament to your love and friendship. Also a moment to include those who couldn't make it in person, but are certainly with us in spirit. There is a special quality to the hours we pass with the people we care for. Our family and friends should never be denied the knowledge of how deeply they have touched our lives. As Shakespeare once said, "I count myself in nothing else so happy as a soul remembering my good friends."

And so Christopher and Joanne stand before you, their family and friends, to begin their journey together as husband and wife.

Ceremony

September 21st is an especially auspicious day for a wedding. It is the Autumn Equinox, a day that has always had a rich place in mythology and ancient traditions. It is one of two days each year when the day and the night are of equal length and nature is in perfect balance. It is the balance imperative to life and to Joanne and Christopher's relationship. It is a time to reflect on the past, give thanks, and celebrate the future. And today we will celebrate the future of a very special couple.

I'd now like to introduce Chris's groomsman, Neal, to read you a fairy tale. . . .

(Neal adds humor to the story of how we became a couple.)

Thank you, Neal.

Joanne and Christopher, I now welcome you to the wonderful world of marriage, an adventure through which you will learn more about yourselves, each other, and the world around you.

You have found in each other the gift of love. Treasure it always. Share your hopes and your dreams. You must practice patience and kindness and know that the answer to disagreement is most often communication. Welcome compromise and embrace your differences. Know how lucky you are to have each other—and never forget that there are no obstacles that can't be overcome by love.

Joanne, you may now take your vows . . .

(Jo's personal vows)

And Christopher . . .

(Chris's personal vows)

Each year on this day, I ask you to reread your vows . . . in memory of today, to celebrate what you have achieved together, and to welcome what lies ahead.

Ring Ceremony

Bradley *(best man)*, may I please have the boat! *(This was our ring cushion because we met on a sailing trip.)*

Thank you.

In ancient times it was believed that the vein in the fourth finger of your left hand lead directly to your heart. So by encircling this finger, your heart is forever touched by the one who loves you.

Let these rings represent your promises to each other. I have cleansed them in salt water so they are as pure as is the love that you share. Let them be a reminder of this moment, your love, and your commitment to each other. May they always be touching your heart.

I Do's

Do you, Joanne, take Christopher to be your lawfully wedded husband, to have and to hold from this day forward, until death do you part?

Joanne: I do. *(Jo puts on Chris's ring.)*

Please repeat after me: With this ring, I thee wed.

Joanne: With this ring, I thee wed.

Do you, Christopher, take Joanne to be your lawfully wedded wife, to have and to hold from this day forward, until death do you part?

Christopher: I do. *(Chris puts on Jo's ring.)*

Please repeat after me: With this ring, I thee wed.

Christopher: With this ring, I thee wed.

I now have the pleasure of introducing two of Chris and Jo's special friends, Sherie and Geoffrey, to sing "Feels like Home."

(Sherie and Geoffrey sing.)

Prayer

May I ask everyone, independent of faiths, to join in this blessing according to your own beliefs and desires. In silent prayer let each of us wish Joanne and Christopher health and happiness always. May they appreciate their togetherness and may they be guided in marriage by honesty, loyalty, and respect. And may their family and friends always be by their side.

Amen

Conclusion

So with the power invested in me by the state of California, I now pronounce you husband and wife. Without further ado, Chris, you may now kiss your bride. . . .

(Bradley hands Chris the glass.)

Let the celebrations continue, for it is with much pleasure that I present to you for the very first time, Mr. and Mrs. Christopher Gartin.

Congratulations!

(break the glass)

Mazel tov!

rings of gold

Add a personal touch to your wedding bands by engraving them. I had "You I love" engraved on my husband's wedding band. You may like to write your wedding date, favorite nicknames, or even simply a word or two that is somehow significant to you both, such as "inspire," "respect," or "forever."

I like to add a little twist to the traditional ring cushion by adding something that's a little unique to each couple and that represents their particular love story. For my wedding, we hung our wedding bands on the mast of a little wooden boat to signify that we met on a sailing trip. One of my couples met at a play, so I photocopied the ticket stubs and collaged them on a simple box that contained their rings. For a garden wedding, I cushioned the rings on a bed of moss packed into a delicate wooden box.

TIMELESS TRADITIONS

Delve into your family's past and search out rituals, traditions, and customs that are unique to your family and heritage, and incorporate them into your ceremony. Google will offer you many paths to follow on this search—just type in "wedding traditions Germany," for example. Adding these sorts of traditions to your service not only pays homage to where you came from, but it is also a great way to deepen your appreciation of the ceremony.

- Did you know that in Africa they literally "tie the knot"? The officiant wraps a length of leather, cord, twine, or vine around the couple to join them in matrimony.

- Buddhist ceremonies open with chanting and an invitation for guests to meditate. You might like to incorporate a version of this, asking your guests to take a moment to reflect on their lives and give thanks.

- You may have seen a groom or two crush a wine glass before hearing "mazel tov" as part of the Jewish tradition. Well, in Japan the groom crushes an egg instead, and with a bare foot!

- "Honi" is a Hawaiian custom. It is the affectionate touching of noses between the bride and groom following the big kiss. Native New Zealanders also embrace this tradition, not only during the wedding ceremony, but often in place of a hug or a handshake.

Ring Ceremony

Not too many people are aware of the origin of the custom of wearing the wedding ring on the left hand once we are married. In ancient Egyptian times, it was believed that the vein in the fourth finger of the left hand led directly to the heart, making it the "vein of love." The ring, with no beginning and no end, also symbolized eternity. It's fun and interesting to include some of these historic details in your ceremony.

Kissing each other's wedding bands before you exchange them is such a romantic gesture.

You may like to exchange family rings during your ceremony to honor the marriage of your parents or other relatives, and then slip on your own wedding bands afterward for the reception.

Take a Moment

Your marriage has been sealed with the infamous kiss, your guests are getting ready to shower you with confetti petals, and you are eager to start the celebrations . . . but wait! This is a perfect opportunity to take a moment to stand and face all your guests. Try to absorb everything; don't feel like you have to rush back down the aisle. This will also give your photographer a great chance to capture your newly wedded excitement.

Try to approach your ceremony with the same love and devotion you have for each other. Your wedding is your day to celebrate the promises you have made and the life you will embark on as husband and wife. Remember that this special day tends to fly by, so take the time to really absorb as much as you can. And above all else, enjoy it!

covered in confetti

Confetti flowers are fun—guests at my own wedding threw a mix of red rose petals and fuchsia orchids after my husband and I said I do. Here are some fun ways to present confetti petals.

- In a little copper bucket with a personalized label
- In a little woven box
- In a paper cone or organza bag tied to the back of each chair
- In miniature Chinese take-out containers

With your ceremony concluded, you'll have walked down the aisle,

confessed your love, committed to each other, and hopefully sealed everything with a kiss.

And so I welcome you to the wonderful world of marriage!

the power of the cocktail hour

Congratulations! You're officially married, and it's time to celebrate!

Traditionally, the cocktail hour follows the ceremony and, in essence,

kick-starts your celebration. Your guests will have just witnessed

your pronouncements of love and will no doubt be eager to celebrate.

Chances are you and your husband will be off having your photos taken for the beginning part of the cocktail hour. This allows your guests to mingle, say their hellos, make introductions, and talk about you!

Imagine it as a "social hour," with cocktails and hors d'oeuvres on the side. And don't take cocktail "hour" too literally either—you might have a cocktail "hour and 15 minutes"!

SETTING THE SCENE

Think of your cocktail hour as a mini event all its own, though it is wise to keep it consistent with your overall wedding vision, no doubt adding a twist here and there. This extra touch may be evidenced in the butler-passed appetizers and cocktails you serve—for example, why not set up a mini tamale bar and serve sangria with it, or serve Asian-inspired hors d'oeuvres along with ginger-infused martinis? Or your music may be what adds the twist—choose a jazz trio or Spanish guitar, perhaps.

It's fun to personalize, and I like hanging signs where I can—without going overboard, of course. I have found cute signs at Cost Plus World Market and at flea markets, too.

One of my favorite ideas is to create a lounge room environment for a couple's cocktail hour, a look that suggests comfort and intimacy. Set up couch clusters. Rent or borrow stand-up lamps, cushions, and coffee tables from a prop house for an extra homey touch.

You might even want to see if your venue will allow you to hang your own artwork. This allows you to really personalize the setting by hanging framed photos of your family or of moments you have shared with each other. You might like to display photos in frames on the coffee tables or set out little pieces of trivia about your relationship—the number of days since you met, who said "I love you" first, or how he proposed, for example. Creating original artwork is also a fun way to personalize your space, and friends and family are always pleased to lend their talents. Or you might decide to rent artwork or mirrors to play up the living-room feeling. If for some reason your venue won't allow you to hang things right on the walls, display artwork on easels instead.

customizing your *cocktail hour*

Following are some fun ways to add personal touches to your cocktail hour.

✦ This cozy lounge room *(top)* was set with royal blue sofas and arm-chairs surrounding coffee tables covered in candles. Throw cushions added to the homey feel, and a wedding photograph of each of the couple's parents was displayed on easels in the corner of the room. Sofas outside can be wonderful, too. I love to set couch clusters and rugs on a grass lawn or a terrace.

✦ This cocktail lounge called for color *(bottom)*. I lined the fireplace mantel with red orchids and placed stacks of art books from the couple's book collection on the coffee table for a personal touch.

✦ I have also placed chalkboards in each corner of the room displaying the bride and groom's cute promises for marriage. One groom wrote "I promise to make you tea each morning" over and over, in school detention style. She wrote "I promise to always kiss you goodnight." Another bride wrote "I will not chase the boys."

✦ As an alternative to couches, sometimes I set up hammocks and daybeds at beachside celebrations and garden weddings.

✦ In the chillier months, I have at times used clay fire pits. These are available at Home Depot as well as most large gardening stores and are ideal for a help-yourself-feast of s'mores, too.

Keep in mind that guests may retreat back to your cocktail area during your reception. Consider utilizing this area to serve sweets, fine cheeses, and after-dinner drinks following the formal reception. Service from an old-fashioned cappuccino machine is always a popular touch.

striking stemware

Research all the glasses that are available to you. Venues often provide complimentary stemware, but consider outsourcing and serving your beverages in something more unique. Visit rental companies and take a trip to such stores as Ikea, Pier 1 Imports, Cost Plus, and restaurant-supply stores to look for inexpensive, interesting glassware. Note that sometimes purchasing unique stemware is almost the same price as renting it.

cheers

Offering a few specialty cocktails can be a great way to kick off your cocktail hour, and it has the added bonus of allowing you to create an impact using color. Watermelon martinis add a burst of red. Tangerine reveals itself in a clementine cosmopolitan or a cantaloupe mojito, and the citrus tones sparkle in lemon drops and apple and honeydew melon martinis. I like to have pre-poured drinks waiting as the cocktail hour commences. Having them butler-passed as guests enter is always a nice touch and prevents a bottleneck at the bar. You might even want to name your cocktails. I had one couple, Lucy and Damien, name their signature drinks "I Love Lucy" and "Damien's Daiquiri."

Cocktails can become little pieces of art if you pay attention to their presentation. Simply adding an interesting garnish or serving the drinks in an unexpected way can make the whole event seem more special. Here are some of my favorites.

Green apple martinis *(left)* are perfect for people with a sweet tooth, like me! Coat the rims in citrus sugar crystals and add a cross section of star fruit for the perfect understated garnish.

Pina coladas might be the perfect cocktail for a summer celebration. I presented these in coconut half shells *(bottom, left)* from www.orientaltradingcompany.com and served them on a wooden tray lined with fresh shaved coconut.

Serve champagne in narrow cylindrical glasses *(bottom, middle)* instead of traditional flutes. These were special-ordered through Classic Party Rentals in Los Angeles. I accent each with a skewer of fresh cranberries, frozen grapes, or blueberries.

These banana Baileys smoothie shots *(bottom, right)* were a huge hit. Served in tiny votives prewrapped in ti leaves and tied with lily grass, they added an unexpected element of fun. Strawberry or papaya vodka smoothies are other popular alternatives.

More Thirst-Quenching Ideas

- A pomegranate martini is a luscious shade of red. Serve with fresh pomegranate seeds at the bottom of the glass if in season. If you're after shades of red, also consider watermelon and blood orange martinis. Red apple martinis and traditional cosmopolitans are also fun. Add berries or a single fresh red rose petal for garnish.

- Set up a vodka bar. Some catering companies will serve shots through ice structures, which makes for a stunning presentation.

- Serve chocolate, mocha, or tiramisu martinis.

- Mojitos are very popular, especially in the warmer months. Add a stick of sugarcane and serve in an old-fashioned tumbler. A twist on a mojito is also popular, such as pomegranate or grapefruit mojitos.

- Shots of soju (a rice-based alcohol that originated in Korea) infused with lychees lend an Asian element. Or sake shots might be the perfect drink for your hour. Both sake and soju are often permitted even at those wedding venues with a beer and wine only liquor code (as they are considered a rice wine). You can also offer sake or soju martinis for variety.

- Another twist on the traditional cocktail hour is to have a wine-tasting bar. You can even add a specialty cheese board for all those fromage connoisseurs.

- Have a nonalcoholic cocktail recipe on hand, fresh juice, or lemonade (in addition to soda) to cater to your underage and non-drinking guests. This way they feel included, too.

- Drinks blended with ice, like frozen margaritas, are great for a hot day.

- Italian ices (the fancy term for snow cones) served in cones make a wonderful impression. You could add a splash of alcohol to these, too.

HORS D'OEUVRES

Your guests were moved to tears by your ceremony, and now hopefully they all have glasses in their hands. Time to start to fill their tummies! Again, remember: Presentation can be everything. Your venue may restrict you in terms of the choices of hors d'oeuvres, but they are almost always willing to mix it up when it comes to presentation. Using cookbooks and entertaining magazines as references can be helpful in conveying to the chef what you're after.

You may like to set up a couple of appetizer stations during your cocktail hour for guests to visit at their leisure.

+ Sushi bars and Bellini bars are a nice treat.

+ Mashed potato martini bars add a tone of fun. Have little scoops of mashed potato served in small martini glasses and top with your favorite garnishes. I love crème fraîche, chives, and caramelized leeks.

+ An oyster bar is great for seafood lovers.

+ Offer miniature quesadillas or tamales from a grill station.

+ A dim sum corner might suit your celebration to a tee.

Be sure to include a variety of options for your tray-passed appetizers—a couple hot, a couple cold, and at least one vegetarian option. I like to offer a choice of at least five hors d'oeuvres. If your venue restricts you to fewer choices, ask them to add a variety of dipping sauces where they can.

You might also like to choose your hors d'oeuvres based on what they mean to you. Bite-size heirloom tomato bruschetta might remind you of your first date at an Italian restaurant. Or lobster tails might make you think of your vacation together in Hawaii—you get the idea.

Let me present some bite-size cocktail treats—some classics as well as some of my favorites, along with a few unusual twists on their presentation.

flower tip

Ask your florist to deliver some blooms and greens to your caterer to accent the serving trays for your hors d'oeuvres. The more resilient blooms are always most appropriate for this purpose.

Bite-Size Burgers

These adorable little burgers are filled with miniature beef patties, Cheddar cheese, tomato, and crispy lettuce. A slice of pickle and a squirt of ketchup complete the package. I like to serve them on little wooden chopping blocks covered in a square of red gingham fabric that I cut with pinking shears. Miniature hot dogs are also a popular choice.

◁ Crab Cakes

Serve crab cakes on simple white china platters and top with a dollop of crème fraîche and slivers of lemon rind. A knot of bear grass is a great, easy garnish. I also like to serve corn fritters, mini tartlets, croquettes, and blue cheese profiteroles with a similar presentation.

▽ Soup Shots

Sweet potato soup shots (try chilled cucumber soup or a gazpacho for the summer) served in sake cups make a great appetizer treat. Serve the cups on a tray covered with forbidden rice. I also like to line trays with tiny pebbles, rose petals, or cranberries. Personalize your serving trays by lining them with paper in colors from your wedding palette.

△ Simple Skewers

These colorful knotted skewers of cherry tomatoes, basil, and bocconcini rolled in chili seasoning rest on a simple wooden serving tray. You may also like to drizzle them with a splash of balsamic vinegar. This simple vegetarian bite should appeal to everyone—well almost!

▽ Have a Ball

Prosciutto-wrapped melon balls presented on miniature forks are the perfect cocktail bite. Garnish with finely chopped chives or add a dollop of mascarpone cheese.

△ Dim Sum

Serve dim sum or pot stickers in authentic Chinese steamers lined with a lattice of tropical leaves. Choose from vegetarian, chicken, shrimp, or beef. Place a little dish of dipping sauce securely in the center.

▷ Shelled Shrimp

Serve ginger-encrusted shrimp from a giant seashell. I love these to be butler-passed. The shell can be filled with floral foam and topped with strands of pearls before the skewers are inserted. Skewers of scallops or lobster medallions also are great special treats.

Treats to Go

Serve your favorite Chinese food in these adorable take-out containers. I recommend buying preassembled containers, as putting them together can be quite a task. These particular take-out containers are from Surfas, my local restaurant-supply store. I also often order from www.beau-coup.com. Personalized chopsticks (also available from Beaucoup) are just right to accompany these mini portions of Chinese chicken salad. These are actually from my wedding. We had "Chris" engraved on one chopstick and "Joanne" on the other. Don't forget to order a few sets for your kitchen keepsakes.

picture perfect

I do believe formal and family photographs are important, as long as
you don't let them keep you from ex-
periencing at least some of your cocktail hour. It is a time filled with
congratulatory hugs and kisses—so
why not make the most of it? To help
expedite your photos and get to your
cocktail hour as soon as possible, prepare a detailed shot list for your photographer in advance. List all the
combinations of family, friends, and
your wedding party that you would
like documented and decide on shoot
locations in advance. And just to be
sure you don't miss out entirely, ask
your catering manager to prepare
some cocktails and an assortment of
hors d'oeuvres to serve you and your
crew during the photo session.

WRITING WISHES

I find the cocktail hour to be the perfect time to introduce your "wish table."
Instead of having guests sign or write their wishes for you in a traditional
guest book, set up a wish table. This can consist of something as simple as
a table dressed in linens on which an oversize hurricane vase (a "wish bowl")
has been set up alongside individual wish cards and pens. Attach a sign to
the hurricane vase, such as "Please Write Your Wishes for Romeo and
Juliet." For wish cards, I like to use small blank sheets of Fabriano paper, an
archive-quality paper available in many art supply stores. You might also like
to use a colored card stock and preprint them with your names and the date.
Colored felt-tip pens can look pretty but don't withstand the test of time as
well as ball point pens. When a wish is written, it joins all the other guests'
wishes in the bowl, so that at the end of your celebration, you should have
a nice little pile of wishes to enjoy. A wish bowl also saves guests from having
to wait in line behind one guest book.

Be creative in choosing your wish bowl. For an autumn wedding, I used a
giant hollowed-out pumpkin and carved the bride and groom's initials in it.
For a wedding at a winery, guests popped their wishes into an old wine
barrel. For a wedding in Mexico, I used a giant sombrero. I have also had
guests pop wish notes into modern wooden boxes, antique hatboxes, and
rustic urns.

A wishing line is also a sweet idea. Hang string between two trees and
ask guests to pin up their wish cards with miniature clothespins. I use "Can
O' Clips" clothespins, which are little wooden clips available from www.art-
suppliesonline.com.

As the evening progresses, I like to casually reposition the wish table close
to the exit so it reminds guests to write a few words before they leave. Along
with having them sign their names, you might also like to ask guests to pose

Wishes in a Bowl

This wish bowl is from Pottery Barn and is lined with strands of white dendrobium orchids. You might also like to use petals or curly willow for the fall, or pinecones or berry branches for the winter. I found a dainty little photo frame in a gift store, printed a sign on my computer to put in it, and then hung it around the neck of the vase with a silver chain.

This leather suitcase was displayed to house wish notes written at one couple's wedding. It later housed all their printed keepsakes.

△ A Wishing Tree

Arrange birch, blossoming branches, or towering curly willow in a large vase or urn. Wrap a sign around the vase asking guests to "Please write your wishes for the newlyweds." Provide pens and wish cards. Before the wedding, hole-punch each card and thread with twine, ribbon, or raffia. Once guests write their wishes, they can hang them from your tree.

▷ A Wishing Canvas

Guests love this alternative to a traditional sign-in table. Display a giant canvas for guests to decorate with their wishes and artwork. Supply paint and pens (I try not to offer anything too messy) and let your guests' creativity shine. I recommend starting your canvas beforehand—maybe paint a background and have some family sign it in advance. This will save any reservation about being the first person to pick up a pen.

for a fun Polaroid and affix that beside their note using a permanent glue stick or double-sided tape. Ask a friend or two to oversee this for you during the cocktail hour if you don't have a coordinator.

Your cocktail hour is a fun time to introduce a photo booth setup, too. You may like to rent the old-fashioned variety for a nostalgic, fun park feel. These make great snapshot albums. Search Google (photo booth rentals along with your city) to find availability in your area.

Wish cards are so much fun to read on your ride to your hotel, the next morning over breakfast, or on your honeymoon. I keep all our wishes in a little wooden box. You may like to slip yours into a keepsake scrapbook.

With wedding wishes being the current topic, I feel compelled to offer you my

congratulatory wishes in advance. So before we turn to the topic of dinner,

imagine me toasting you with a mango mojito in hand . . .

"May your life together become your fairy tale. Wishing you so many wonderful things."

dinner and dancing

A beautiful ceremony, followed by a fabulous cocktail hour—now it's time to dine.

Or, maybe you've mixed up that order and held your cocktail hour

prior to your ceremony, then changed into your wedding gown

before walking down the aisle?

Although the majority of weddings take place in the evening, you might want to consider a daytime event—perhaps, for example, a morning ceremony followed by a champagne brunch, or a midday wedding rolling into a divine luncheon.

Daytime weddings are usually much more affordable than evening ceremonies. One of my all-time favorite midday weddings was a beach barbecue boasting jerk chicken, corn on the cob, and giant seafood kebabs. Elaborate cocktail receptions are also becoming very popular as are evenings of decadent desserts. Whatever time of day you decide to celebrate, let your reception be filled with everything wonderful.

SETTING THE SCENE

I find the easiest way to begin designing a reception is by mapping out where your tables will be positioned (and your dance floor, if you are planning to kick up your heels!). You may want to seat your guests either at traditional round tables or at banquet tables or even at square tables for eight. You may even want to use a combination of all three. I find that once this layout is decided upon, it becomes easier to focus on your individual table designs.

Ask the staff at your venue whether such items as linens, china, stemware, and silverware are available to you through them. This can often be included in your quote at no additional charge, so you may as well take advantage of it!

Linens

Consider renting specialty linens or even just overlays or table runners. I love to work with www.bbjlinen.com, who will ship anywhere in the United States and include a return bag and a prepaid FedEx slip for an easy next-business-day pickup. You might choose to keep your tables classic-looking by using standard off-white linens and then introduce a specialty napkin, colored or with detailed edges, that can give the look a little twist.

If you fold one napkin as you would like all of the napkins folded and give it to your event manager or caterer to use as a sample, they will usually fold them for you accordingly. If they won't fold them, ask if you can pick up the napkins (or have them delivered to you) a couple of days beforehand and fold them yourself.

- Roll your napkins and tie them with a few strands of greenery, such as lily or bear grass. You can usually do this a day or two beforehand—it's wise to test this first because there is really no way of knowing just how fresh the greenery is.

- Rent or scout for custom napkin rings. Another idea is to tie napkins with a knot of ribbon or raffia, a natural fiber.

- Pocket-fold your napkins (sometimes called a tri-fold). This creates a built-in pocket in the napkin that is a perfect place to tuck in a menu, name card, or even your silverware.

- You may also like to accent your place settings by tucking a fresh flower or a pretty leaf into each pocket-folded napkin. This, of course, often needs to be done on the day of your celebration to avoid wilting.

- I often have runners custom-made to dress banquet tables. This can be as simple as making a trip to my local fabric store to choose the material and then dropping it off with my seamstress. If you don't have a seamstress, ask at the fabric store—they are usually very helpful. You will want to choose fabric that is easy to sew—if you aren't sure, take a fabric sample to the person who will be making the runners for you for their approval.

China

I find that using simple white square plates (which you can rent) adds a modern touch. Triangular plates look great for salads and desserts. Eclectic cups and saucers (even mismatched) can be perfect for a garden wedding or even just for a cappuccino or dessert bar. In addition to specialty china rentals, a trip to Ikea, Pier 1 Imports, or Cost Plus often produces interesting and affordable china.

my favorite *dinner tables*

Reception with a View

Held at a private home, this Hollywood Hills celebration overlooked the entire city. Round tables were set with white hemstitch linens and centerpieces overflowing with burgundy calla lilies, dark pink orchids, and chocolate cosmos. Dinner menus were calligraphed and included a special note from the bride and groom expressing how grateful they were for the love and support of their family and friends. (Make sure menus are easy to read since they are often read in candlelight and by some elderly guests.)

◁ Feeling at Home

I transformed this couple's lawn into an elegant, cozy winter dining room. Ivory carpet was scattered with petals, the tent ceiling was draped with chocolate brown velvet and twinkle lights. Long tables were set with latte-colored linens and brown woolen table runners. Vases lined with petals and filled with hand-opened red roses were placed down each table along with squares of votives.

▽ A Tuscan Touch

Reminiscent of a wine cellar, these grand tables were lined with assorted wines from the bride and groom's personal collection, a variety of candles, and dozens of full-bloomed terra-cotta and leonidas roses. Hanging mirrors on the walls opened the room up—you may like to purchase these and hang them in your home afterward. I have also rented mirrors from prop houses and antique stores.

△ Entirely Elegant

For this modern all-white wedding, long tables were set with off-white linens. A runner of vases filled with fresh white orchids dressed every table; for seating, I selected a combination of off-white dining chairs and giant white couches. Decadent crystal chandeliers hung from above. Make sure the arrangements are not so high that guests sitting opposite one another cannot converse.

Wall to Wall

As I suggested in the section on cocktail areas, you might like to bring in wall hangings or sconces to personalize your reception room. Artwork and photographs often work well. You might like to borrow some, rent them, or put your talents to the test with originals! Blown-up framed photographs can look amazing. Printing photos on fabric (try Kinko's or your local printers) and then staple-gunning them to canvases can look great (and it's a fun project, too!). Hanging these in your home afterward or giving them to family and friends as gifts will add to the memories.

For one wedding, I lined a hallway entrance to a ballroom with a dozen giant colored canvases resting on easels. I hand-painted them and wrote out the love story of how the bride and groom met, fairy-tale-style, beginning with "once upon a time" and ending with "happily ever after." Of course, this doesn't need to be done on such a grand scale. Allow some time for guests to enjoy such a display on their entrance.

Note that clever lighting can change the whole tone of a room. Inquire about using a lighting company. I love to incorporate strings of twinkle lights, lanterns, and/or clusters of candles if I can. If you will be dining under a tent, look into renting lanterns or light fixtures to hang from the ceiling. Ikea has some fabulous giant stand-up lights that I've used for ambient lighting at evening events.

MENU

Designing your menu can be fun and also often a mouth-watering experience. At most of my weddings a formal three-course meal is served, including a starter, an entrée, and dessert.

Starter

The first course most often consists of a salad selected by you on behalf of your guests. For weddings in the colder months, you instead might opt for a hot soup to start your meal. An autumn wedding might call for butternut squash soup served in white pumpkin shells alongside giant loaves of sunflower bread. You might even want to use a family recipe. At one winter wedding, for example, we served the bride's grandmother's famous chili corn chowder. Alternatively (or in addition to your salad course), present an appetizer course. We selected grilled baby artichokes to serve at a Carmel, California, celebration. Corn fritters are yummy and are ideal for the fall. A classic tower of ahi tuna or portobello mushrooms is sure to impress.

Entrée

I find that there are four general ways to tackle your main meal. Your choice is often dictated by preference, budget, or catering restrictions.

- You might offer your guests a choice of entrées the evening of the reception.

- You can choose what is often referred to as a split entrée, which means you select two different but complementary meals and a half portion of each is served to each guest with the accompaniments acting as a divider. Filet mignon and lobster tail is a favorite combination. New York steak and blackened cod is another possible choice.

- You might include a menu card with your invitation, which invites guests to select from a choice of entrées. Sending their selections to your caterer ahead of time is typically the least expensive option.

- You can choose one meal on your guest's behalf and have a backup vegetarian option for guests who don't like or can't eat the primary offering. I always have my couples select a silent vegetarian option. This simply means that the dish is not offered on the menu, but is available upon request. Unless you know that you have a large vegetarian crowd, allowing for 10 percent of your guests to ask for a vegetarian meal is typically quite safe.

Dessert

I have such a sweet tooth that I had to give dessert its own chapter! See page 124 for all of my favorite—and most popular—ideas.

painting plates

I like to think of the dinner plate as a blank canvas. Creating your menu is not only about the taste of the food—it is also about the presentation. Keep this in mind when planning your dinner menu, especially with regard to your choice of china.

- Remember to consider color combinations when choosing your accompaniments. An entrée of miso-infused halibut, pureed parsnips, and sautéed leeks, for instance, tends to look a little bland. Replacing the pureed parsnips with summer squash and the leeks with baby carrots and asparagus tips would introduce some color.

- Flip through food magazines and tear out photographs of food presentations you like. Add these to your wedding scrapbook as a guide for your chef or planner.

- Try to stay away from choosing foods with very strong tastes. Filet mignon topped with a caviar glaze or a caper chutney may not appeal to the majority. If you are determined to offer something a little strong, serve it on the side!

MUSIC

A band can be wonderful. Maybe you'd like a blues band or a big band with lots of brass instruments. An element of classic rock and roll might be your style, or you may have something more contemporary in mind, such as a soul-influenced band. Some couples prefer a DJ to keep things moving on the dance floor. This is purely a question of personal preference (although sometimes budget will dictate, as hiring a DJ usually costs considerably less than hiring a band). Whatever your choice, I recommend making a list of all the songs you'd like played. Just as important, list the songs you don't want to play at your wedding.

Some couples opt for a variety of music at their reception—maybe a grand piano for dinner, a big band for dancing, and a DJ to close out the night! My favorite DJ also teams up with percussionists to create a live-music feel but for a fraction of the price. This is something you might like to surprise guests with after dinner.

Dance Floor

Casting a pattern of light on your dance floor adds a great effect. Choose from a leaf design, something more stylized, or personalize by asking for your initials. I had one couple write out a romantic note to each other, and I had that cast upon the dance floor. It was very subtle, but they both knew that they were dancing on love letters!

Tired Toes

For all those ladies dancing in heels, you might like to offer a shoe check area—self-serve! I often buy little slippers from Chinatown in assorted sizes so that female guests can kick off their uncomfortable high heels and put on comfy dancing shoes (or try ordering online from www.asianideas.com).

FOLLOW A FLOW

A preplanned timeline will guide your vendors and whoever will be "hosting" your reception. (By a "host," I refer to the person who will introduce speeches and make announcements. This master of ceremonies can be a friend or family member, the band leader, or the DJ.) Remember throughout the course of the festivities that this timeline is just a guide for how your celebration should flow—if you dance a little longer than expected between courses, that's okay!

I like to start my receptions by bringing everyone to the dance floor. This initial energy sets the tone for the rest of the night. The perfect way to do this is to make a grand entrance as husband and wife and go directly to the dance floor for your first dance. Have your DJ or band leader then welcome your bridal party to join you on the dance floor, followed closely by an invitation for all guests to dance. (Now is the perfect time for the hora if you would like to include this Jewish custom.) After 10 to 15 minutes of kicking up your heels, you can invite guests to return to their seats by announcing something like, "Ladies and gentlemen, the first course will now be served." At this time I like to have a welcome speech, traditionally given by the father of the bride. The first course typically follows. In between courses is a perfect time for other speeches and tributes. I advise my couples to limit speeches here to three or four depending on their length. If you don't have a coordinator to take care of this for you, I advise assigning a friend or family member to make sure all the important people are present before announcing speeches—it would be horrible to be in the powder room while your maid of honor is waiting to toast you!

Following the main course, I like to introduce the father-daughter/mother-son dance. It is the perfect opportunity to welcome guests back to the dance floor.

To some, the cake cutting signifies the end of the evening. Each wedding is different in its flow, so there is no set rule for when to cut your cake. It's a delicate balance between not disturbing the energy on the dance floor and not leaving it for too late in the event. If you and your husband would like to say a few words, I find that doing so immediately following the cake cutting is the perfect moment.

Dinner and dancing may be well under way, but I do hope

you have left room for dessert. With full bellies and tired toes,

let's treat ourselves to sweets.

sweet treats

I am proud to confess I have the ultimate sweet tooth.

My idea of a perfect dessert is a little bit of everything,

and I like to try to incorporate that into my events.

I love to let my creativity flow when it comes to planning desserts.

Wow your guests with decadent soufflés or bring back memories with Rice Krispies treats

and ice-cream sandwiches . . . It's all about saving the best 'til last!

DESSERT LOUNGE

If you have decided to retreat back to your cocktail lounge following dinner and dancing, serve bite-size desserts at the coffee tables. You might also like to scatter about bowls of your favorite chocolates and candies.

A cappuccino machine is always a big hit. Serve traditional lattes and old-fashioned hot chocolate with marshmallows. Offer crystal sugar stirrers and cookies on the side (I love shortbread and classic chocolate chip).

Another option is to set up a scotch bar or offer a selection of dessert wines, port, and brandy. Pair these drinks with candied pecans, dried nectarines, champagne grapes, or figs, and an assortment of imported cheeses and crackers. It's nice to label your cheeses by printing little name tags and attaching them with toothpicks.

You might like to set up a crepe station with these delicious French treats made-to-order. My favorite is a crepe sprinkled with sugar and a squeeze of lemon. Fried bananas are another popular addition. Brandy snaps and traditional vanilla ice cream make great accompaniments.

BITE-SIZE SWEETS

Instead of choosing one dessert to follow your main course, ask about offering assorted bite-size treats. Place a selection of miniature sweets on a platter or cake tier at each table. You may also like to have some desserts butler-passed for those guests who are already up and about. I like to include a chocolate choice, something a little simpler such as mini cheesecakes or crème brûlée, and something fruity, like a lemon tart—this way you should satisfy almost everyone's tastebuds. Here are some of my favorite miniature treats. Again, I love to focus on presentation.

◁ Perfect Profiteroles

Profiteroles, served in self-standing Chinese spoons and coated in a decadent chocolate sauce with sprigs of fresh mint, are my ultimate bite-size treats.

▽ Tiramisu Towers

Serve tiramisu in shot glasses and top with a chocolate swirl. Espresso mugs are also well suited for this little treat.

△ Mini Milkshakes

These strawberry milkshakes are a fun way to finish the evening. You might even like to set up a milkshake counter.

▽ Just Jello

This nostalgic treat is sure to stir up some childhood memories. I like to serve mini portions of gelatin in shot glasses or mini martini glasses such as these, available from www.beaucoup.com. Serve with a dollop of fresh whipped cream or ice cream.

△ Some Like Sorbet

Present passion fruit sorbet in the shells of passion fruit. Lemon, coconut, and tangelo sorbets also look perfect in their shells.

▷ Healthy Treats

I like to include a little something especially for the health-conscious, even if it's just long-stemmed strawberries. These skewers of cubed pineapple, watermelon, and cantaloupe look adorable when presented in a box of wheat grass.

More Sweet Bite-Size Ideas

Here are some more of my most popular just-a-taste treats.

+ Crème brûlée in self-standing spoons

+ Bread and butter puddings (or banana bread pudding) in mini ramekins

+ Toblerone chocolate mousse (Snickers mousse is also a favorite)

+ Mini ice-cream sandwiches

+ Tiny apple tarts

+ Miniature strawberry shortcakes or cheesecakes

If you'd prefer to serve a traditional dessert, you might want to stay away from anything that must be served hot or anything that can melt, like ice creams or sorbet, unless they are served immediately after dinner and before guests are dancing. No one wants to return to an apple tart swimming in a bowl of ice-cream soup!

we all scream for ice cream

+ An ice cream stand on a summer's evening is a great treat for your guests after dinner. Serve ice cream in cones or cups, or try a sundae-making station.

+ Fruity sorbets are a healthy alternative.

+ Homemade Kahlúa creamsicles and vodka cranberry popsicles have been big hits at some weddings I've planned.

+ Italian ices also make a great after-dinner refreshment.

wedding cake wonders

If there is ever going to be a day when you can have your cake and eat it, too, then this is it! Not only is your cake a sweet treat for you and your guests, it is also yet another opportunity to add a personal touch. One of my brides insisted on having Oreo cookies at her celebration, so we filled her traditional white wedding cake with a center filling of white chocolate mousse blended with crumbled Oreos—this nostalgic touch was a huge hit! Chunks of Toblerone or Heath bars work well also.

Wedding cakes can be works of art. I worked with one of my favorite cake designers to create these three simply stunning towers of confection.

This Asian-inspired cake *(opposite)* is covered in blush fondant and wrapped in a cherry blossom branch with delicate blooms, all hand-crafted from sugar.

Wrapped in edible crystals molded from sugar, this platinum wedding cake *(top)* is striking and elegant.

Inspired by a Monique Lhuillier gown, this latte-colored masterpiece *(bottom)* is covered in rows of molded ivory sugared lace.

my take
on a wedding cake

All about Orchids
I scattered this grand tower with dark brown and dark pink cymbidium orchids. It sits on a cake box lined with blush pink dupioni silk and a band of chocolate brown woven straw ribbon.

◁ Bougainvillea Bliss

I love this wedding cake's bold contrast of smooth white buttercream frosting and fuchsia flowers. I displayed this cake on a wooden box that I lined with bamboo slats (which came from window blinds I cut down to size) and filled with bougainvillea blooms. A handful of blooms also graces the top tower.

▽ Butterfly Kisses

Gold butterflies are the focal point of this fondant wedding cake. Each tier is lined in a band of gold-embroidered ribbon that I found at my local fabric store and delicate feathered butterflies, which appear to be resting from flight.

△ Wrapped in Ivy

This cake, from a summer celebration, is encircled by garden ivy and kumquats, which perfectly capture the season's grandeur.

Cake Toppers

I love to display fresh flowers on the top of the wedding cakes I decorate, but if you are looking for something sentimental, there just may be the perfect cake topper in your family. You might also personalize your cake by incorporating details unique to you. One of the brides I worked with met her husband while scuba diving. They placed two delicate Swarovski crystal fish among the flowers on the top of their cake. Another couple wanted to incorporate a photo that had been taken of them together when they were in grade school. I photocopied the picture, reduced it, and made it into a simple two-sided flag that stood 5 inches from the top tier.

Fabulous Flavors

You can choose a different flavor for each layer of your cake and put a twist on the fillings—after all, they say variety is the spice of life! Here are some mouth-watering combinations.

- Old-fashioned chocolate cake with a caramelized pecan ganache center
- Traditional vanilla cake with a fresh berry, whipped cream, and crumbled meringue or lemon curd center
- A tiramisu mud cake with a white chocolate center
- Carrot cake or banana cake with a cream cheese and maple syrup frosting
- Red velvet cake with a cream cheese mousse center
- Coconut cake with a buttercream center blended with fresh coconut shavings

Don't feel like you must have a wedding cake, either. For my wedding, we had a dessert tower instead. I wrapped the pillars in orchid leis and displayed assorted mini chocolate mousse towers on tropical leaves.

Alternatively, you might like to have your cake double as your dessert. Accent each cake plate with a fresh flower, rose petals, or a long-stemmed strawberry, for example. There may not be much time to focus on presentation with so many pieces of cake to be sliced so quickly, but these little additions can certainly make a big difference.

If you would like to display your cake outdoors, consider weather elements and any insect issues. To keep ants away from your cake, lightly scatter teaspoonfuls of sugar about the grass around your cake table. If it's very hot outside, think about featuring your cake indoors or ask your baker about delivering the cake chilled and as late as possible so that it's at the perfect temperature by the time you cut it.

CUT THE CAKE

It may seem silly, but it is often wise to briefly practice your cake cutting. It can be slightly embarrassing to fumble about in front of a full audience. Traditionally, the bride stands to the left of her husband and takes the cake knife in her right hand, and then he places his hand over hers. Together, they cut a small slice of cake from the bottom layer (this is usually the easiest tier to attack) and place it on a plate. He offers his bride a bite, and then it's his turn to indulge as she offers him a taste. It's a good idea to have napkins handy. Using your hands is quite acceptable in this case.

You might like to cut your cake using the same knife that your parents or someone else in your family used at their wedding. If there isn't a special cake knife in the family, buy yourselves a little wedding gift and start your own tradition! Engrave the knife with your names and your wedding date and then pass it down through the family for those to follow. I like to remind my couples to make a wish for themselves just before the knife hits the bottom.

I hope you enjoyed browsing through this little library of confectionery wonders.

Round cakes or square, two tiers, maybe four . . . tarts and truffles and mousse and more . . .

Whatever treats you choose as sweets, I'm sure they'll never be quite as sweet

as the love that surrounds your special day.

gracious gifts

After all your planning, there are sure to be people to thank:

your family, your bridesmaids, his groomsmen, out-of-town guests

who traveled to share your day with you, and friends

who offered their help and support.

When it comes to gift giving, it really *is* the thought that counts.

It's nice to let this idea influence your planning of the entire event.

These pages offer some **thoughtful ways** to say thank you.

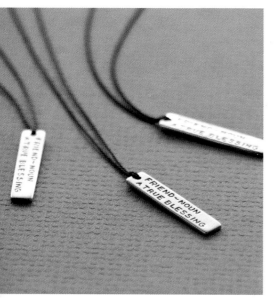

Jewelry is a great gift. I designed the delicate pendants shown here and had them made by Claude Morady Jewelers in Beverly Hills. They say, "friend ~ noun, a true blessing" dictionary-style. You might also like to engrave pendants with something unique for each maid, such as a word of inspiration, a Chinese character, or their favorite number.

GIFTS FOR THE WEDDING PARTY

It is customary to give a little something to members of your wedding party. And don't feel like you have to buy an identical gift for everyone. Choosing a unique gift for each special person allows you to really personalize.

Your Maids

These women are your family and best friends. They have all, in their own way, touched your heart with their love and friendship. This is your opportunity to thank them. Here are some ideas.

✦ Present each maid with a journal embossed with her name (or a book that you think she will love) and fill the opening page with all the reasons you are grateful she is in your life. You might also like to write a poem—an original or an old favorite—in the journal or book. I gave one of my bridesmaids a copy of *Charlotte's Web* and a bookmark I made from a strip of old photo booth pictures we had taken when we were teenagers.

✦ Consider giving each maid a photo album or scrapbook; the inside cover is an ideal place to write a note. Your maids can fill it with photos from your wedding.

✦ Look around for a purse to complement each maid. They don't all have to be the same as long as the styles are complementary—it's wonderful if each purse reflects each maid's individual style. Ideally, they can carry the purses with them at your wedding.

+ A trip to a spa or a salon for a manicure and pedicure is a girly outing you can all enjoy together.

+ Waterproof mascara and tissues make a cute little trinket gift.

His Men

Finding gifts for the guys is always a little more difficult. Gifts such as cigar boxes and cutters and silver hip flasks are always classic. Here are a couple of less traditional options.

+ Tickets to a sports game

+ Pre-wedding massages

+ Books that have been personalized with a note on the inside cover

+ A game of golf

+ Ties to wear at your wedding

+ Subscriptions to their favorite magazines

+ Gadgets like iPods or digital cameras, if you're in the mood to really splurge

Flower Girls

Depending on the age of your flower girls, treating them to a little hair and makeup sitting can be a success. Try some lip gloss, or a little blush with a sparkle. Organize a visit to a salon for a fancy hairdo and paint her nails with just a clear coat with some glitter. Alternatively, buy little ballet slippers or fairy wings and attach a special thank-you note. Jewelry, such as a little locket, can also be a big hit.

Page Boys or Ring Bearers

Buying for boys can be a little more challenging than buying for your flower girls. A watch is often a good idea, or you might ask their moms for help in selecting their latest must-have toy, such as a video game.

Your Parents

You may like to give a special gift to each of your parents to thank them for their love and support and all of their help, or for paying for your wedding! Some great ideas include:

+ A journal filled with all the wonderful memories you have of your childhood and the time leading up to your wedding

+ A photo album embossed with a note such as "for the memories to come"

+ Tickets to the theater or the opera

+ A weekend away

+ Jewelry for Mom and cuff links for Dad

WELCOME GIFTS FOR YOUR GUESTS

It's a lovely idea to have a little something waiting for each guest in their hotel room upon their arrival. I love to make up boxes and fill them with goodies and a personalized note from the bride and groom. You may also like to enclose an itinerary to remind guests of any wedding events, along with a few recommendations for places to dine and sites to see in your area. I think it is sweet to list these under "The Bride's Favorites" and "The Groom's Favorites."

You may like to spend some time in gift stores looking for the perfect presentation to capture the style of your wedding. Keep in mind that guests are traveling: Don't choose anything so large that they can't possibly take it home with them. Here are some of my most-requested welcome treats.

welcome sack

I found these great canvas totes at www.blissweddingsmarket.com. I personalized them using fabric paint and a stencil of the Chinese symbol for love. Personalizing with iron-on transfers is fun, too. You can also have your wedding date and location embroidered on fabrics. This goodie bag is home to:

✦ Bottles of Voss water
  (www.vosswater.com)

✦ Lindt chocolate balls
  (www.worldwidechocolate.com)

✦ A Chinese take-out container filled
  with a decadent assortment of dried
  fruits and nuts

✦ A little book on feng shui

✦ Incense from
  www.beau-coup.com

hats off to you

Hats can be a fun way to package things. I used sombreros for a wedding in Mexico. For a summer wedding, I filled this straw hat with:

✦ Bottles of sparkling water

✦ A bag of pretzels, which I repackaged and sealed with a miniature clothespin

✦ Apple-scented bubble bath

✦ A disposable camera (I like to provide ones with black-and-white film for more artistic photos)

✦ Mouthwatering handmade toffees from Valerie Confections (www.valerieconfections.com)

all about orange

Fill a fun box (this one is from www.kolo.com) or a kraft paper bag with goodies that you've chosen in a specific color scheme. Here, I went with an orange theme including:

✦ Tangerine-flavored sodas

✦ Miniature marshmallows, which were repackaged in little baggies and sealed with a personalized label from www.myownlabels.com

✦ Jelly Belly jelly beans packed in miniature paint cans with a personalized label

✦ A pair of tangerines, which are healthy and likely to survive any minor accidental squashing. I like to present these in little burlap bags. I found these bags at www.blissweddingsmarket.com.

hung with care

These welcome pouches were made by the bride's mother and hung perfectly from the bedposts in each guest's hotel room. They included:

✦ Old-fashioned kettle potato chips

✦ A copy of a gossip magazine, scrolled and tied with string

✦ Bottles of water

✦ A Kinder's chocolate surprise

travel treats

For guests who are traveling a long way, splurge and fill little suitcases with treats such as:

✦ Candied popcorn

✦ Bottles of Jones soda—you can personalize these with photos at www.myjones.com

✦ A deck of fun preprinted cards called *52 Great Travel Tips,* written by Lynn Gordon and published by Chronicle Books—you can order them at www.barnesandnoble.com

✦ A travel game such as dominoes

nostalgic knickknacks

This bucket of goodies greeted guests at an East Hampton wedding. They enjoyed:

+ Salt-and-vinegar chips

+ Bottles of old-fashioned lemonade

+ Candies

+ Gum

+ A Rubik's Cube, for a touch of nostalgia

More Welcome Treat Ideas

+ A deck of playing cards can be personalized with an image or your names and the date. Order them at www.customplayingcards.com.

+ Sunscreen and flip-flops are perfect for a sunny location

+ Your favorite novel

+ A guide to the city

+ A bottle of wine is perfect for a vineyard wedding

+ If the rooms have fireplaces, include marshmallows to toast and a sachet of hot chocolate.

+ Decadent bath products

+ A pair of terry cloth slippers

+ Personalized T-shirts

+ Travel puzzles, or maybe a jigsaw made out of a special photo

FAVORS

The best gift your guests can take from your wedding is the wonderful memory of the love and beauty they experienced. A take-home favor is a nice touch, but certainly not a must. Consider these ideas.

+ Tray-pass ready-to-eat midnight snacks as guests leave—grilled cheese bites and mini cheeseburgers can create quite a frenzy!

+ See if a Coffee Bean truck can come to your location so guests can enjoy a latte on the ride home.

+ Arrange for your guests to take home your centerpieces.

If you want to give your guests a little something special as they leave, consider the favors on the following pages that they are sure to love.

all packed up

Using individual labels to personalize is always a nice touch—I often order from www.myownlabels.com. Or, you can personalize the gifts themselves with embroidery—have your name or initial sewn onto one slipper, and your fiancé's on the other, for example. Here are some more ideas for presenting your welcome gifts.

+ Beach bags or straw bags

+ Sun hats or cowboy hats

+ Chinese steamers

+ Buckets (perfect for a beach location!)

+ Watering cans (sweet for a garden wedding)

+ Bamboo boxes or wooden boxes (www.dufeckwood.com)

lolly lineup

Let guests participate in making their own take-home treats. On a long table, set up giant glass jars filled with your favorite sweets. Monochromatic goodies look great! Attach labels to each jar to let guests know the contents. Offer each guest a little box or bag (Chinese take-out containers are sweet, too) and a little scoop so they can help themselves before they leave. You might also like to personalize the bag. These red sweets are primarily from www.candydirect.com and include Twizzlers, hot tamales, Swedish Fish, apple sours, lollipops, and Lindt chocolate balls. You might also like to include all red M&M's (they can be personalized with your date or initials, too) and cherry Sour Patch Kids.

newlywed news

Offer a copy of the early edition of the morning newspaper. You might like to pair this with a sweet treat. Order these well in advance from a local newsstand and have them picked up and scrolled the morning of your wedding.

midnight snack

Try a little take-out box filled with a midnight snack. These boxes and the personalized labels are available from www.myownlabels.com. You can fill them with such treats as a bagel and cream cheese, chocolate croissants, mini chocolate milks, doughnuts, doughnut holes, bottles of chilled Starbuck's Frappuccinos, homemade cookies, bottles of fresh juice, or even peanut butter and jelly sandwiches! If you have a valet service, ask them to put the snacks in each guest's car as a little surprise.

perfect packaging

Presentation can be everything. Even a simple handful of chocolate-covered raisins can make a grand impression if displayed well. I have repackaged Rice Krispies treats in little baggies sealed with ribbon or a personalized label. I often buy from these Web sites when ordering favor packaging:

www.beau-coup.com

www.blissweddingsmarket.com

www.myownlabels.com

www.orientaltradingcompany.com

www.weddingthings.com

Fill little tins with goodies, then add personalized labels *(top)*. Try candies, jelly beans, giant gum balls, mints or Tic Tacs, or even personalized M&M's. Loose-leaf tea is also a nice option. For a real surprise, place a penny and a lottery ticket inside each tin!

These jars are filled with homemade candied pecans *(bottom)*. A delicious, crowd-pleasing treat, these sweet nuts are as easy as pie to make in an afternoon. For each pound of halved pecans, place the pecans, $\frac{1}{3}$ cup butter, and $\frac{1}{3}$ cup maple syrup in a nonstick frying pan. Cook over medium-high heat, stirring constantly, until the pecans have lightly browned. Allow them to cool before packaging.

KEEPSAKES

Your journey through the wonderful world of weddings will eventually come to an end. You and your groom might want to treat yourselves to a lovely box where you can keep mementos that you have collected along the way. Gathering them may seem a little daunting right now, but trust me, it's well worth the effort. My husband and I take out our little box of treasures at every anniversary.

Scrapbook. Fill a scrapbook or keep a folder with magazine clippings to reference when visiting vendors. Highlight gowns you love, flowers that impress, food presentations that capture your eye, and invitations that you're drawn to. Create a visual collage of all the elements that belong in your fairy-tale wedding.

Journal. Keeping a journal over your engagement makes a fantastic read in years to come. A honeymoon journal is great, too. Make entries about what you did each day, along with reliving the memories of your wedding. So much happens in a day that your wedding can seem like a giant happy dream. Utilize the free time on your honeymoon to capture everything in writing while it is still fresh in your mind.

Receipts. Try to keep some receipts—in 20 years, your wedding will seem like a bargain. But you don't have to limit yourself to receipts from the wedding: Looking through ticket stubs from movies you saw together or the receipt from the dinner the night he proposed can make sweet memories. You might like to do this for your honeymoon, too.

Stationery. Keep a sample of all your stationery items from save-the-dates and invitations through to your thank-you notes, as well as all of your reply cards and wedding wishes. Print out any congratulatory e-mails and keep a list of all the friends and family who celebrated with you. It's surprising how quickly you can forget some of the faces that watched you walk down the aisle.

Photo Friendly. Take photos as you're planning. Shots of you looking at your venue, trying on dresses at the bridal boutique, choosing flowers, shopping for wedding bands, or tasting your cake are great for your scrapbook. Ask a friend to take some Polaroids for you throughout your celebration. This way, you can have some instant memories to enjoy before you get your photos developed.

In Print. Keep a copy of the newspaper from the day you were married. You can also arrange for your marriage to be announced in the paper.

Vows to Keep. Keep a written copy of the promises you made to each other. You might like to read them again on each anniversary in memory of your wedding day.

anniversary gifts

If you'd like to follow tradition, here is a list of some of the gifts suggested for your first 10 years, along with some ideas. Believe it or not, diamonds don't make their appearance until your 60th anniversary!

First: *Paper* Tickets to a concert or plane tickets to a second honeymoon, a love letter, a journal, personalized stationery, an artbook, a framed photograph, and if you haven't yet put together your wedding photo album, this is the perfect gift to each other.

Second: *Cotton* Underwear, clothing, bed linens, a posy of cotton puffs, a romantic picnic in the cotton fields

Third: *Leather* Handbag, wallet, luggage (could be paired with a little weekend getaway), shoes, watch with a leather strap, a club chair, a photo album

Fourth: *Silk or fruit/flowers* Lingerie, camisole, silk boxers, sheets, a tie, a trip to an orchard or a weekend amongst grapevines at a vineyard, breakfast in bed (fresh fruit and granola), a potted orchid in an antique vase, lunch in a botanical garden

Fifth: *Wood* Dinner by a wood-burning fireplace, wood furniture, art displayed in a wooden frame

Sixth: *Candy or iron* Classic sweets or a decadent surprise—maybe pair candy up with a movie—light fixtures for the home, a wine rack, golf clubs

Seventh: *Copper or wool* New copper numbers for your house or apartment, a hand-knitted scarf, or a pair of sheepskin slippers

Eighth: *Bronze* Look into buying some art—a sculpture, for instance—or bronze yourself on a sun-filled getaway.

Ninth: *Pottery* A sculpture; maybe you'd like to take a pottery class together or buy some new pottery plates for the cabinet.

Tenth: *Tin or aluminum* I don't know about you, but after 10 years of marriage, I'm actually hoping for a little more than something tin. I suggest wrapping jewels in a tin box or a piece of aluminum foil.

well, miss bride,

The time has come to set you free. May the time you spend planning your wedding be filled with wonder. Enjoy the creativity that can transform your celebration. Open your imagination and let your personal style shine through. Bring thought and passion to your day. Take my ideas, mold them into your own, and let them make your wedding truly one-of-a-kind. And through everything, remember to cherish the love that has brought you here! After all, that's what your wedding is all about. May you always be in love, may luck stand by your side, and may an angel always be holding your hand.

Enjoy, Jo

resources

Contact the following companies to purchase or learn more about many of the items mentioned in this book.

All About Dance.com
PO Box 2055
Kingston, PA 18704
www.allaboutdance.com
800-775-0578
Ballet slippers

Art Supplies Online
www.artsuppliesonline.com
800-967-7367
Miniature clothespins, easel backs, paints, photo albums, and other art supplies

Asian Ideas
412 West Applegate Avenue
Suite A
Pen Argyl, PA 18072
www.asianideas.com
888-38-IDEAS (888-384-3327)
Chinese slippers

BBJ Linen
www.bbjlinen.com
Specialty linens for rent

Beaucoup Wedding Favors
www.beau-coup.com
877-988-2328
Wedding favors and packaging, including take-out containers, personalized chopsticks, miniature martini glasses, and incense, as well as decorations and wedding party gifts

Bliss! Weddings Market
PO Box 363
Woodbury, NY 11797
www.blissweddingsmarket.com
866-445-4405
Wedding favors, gifts, and packaging, including canvas tote bags, burlap bags, and ribbon

Candy Direct.com

www.candydirect.com

Online retailer of all types of candy, including retro favorites, movie candy, mints, and chocolates

Cocktail Umbrellas.com

2020 Bathurst Street, Suite #4

Toronto, ON M5P 3L1

Canada

www.cocktailumbrellas.com

800-296-5408

Assorted cocktail umbrellas

Custom Playing Cards.com

Kardwell International

PO Box 33

Mattituck, NY 11952

www.customplayingcards.com

800-233-0828

Personalized playing cards

Dufeck Manufacturing Company

210 Maple Street

PO Box 428

Denmark, WI 54208-0428

www.dufeckwood.com

888-603-9663

Bamboo and wooden boxes

Kolo Retail

PO Box 572

Windsor, CT 06095-0572

www.kolo.com

888-636-5656

Photo albums, storage boxes, and accessories

My Jones Soda Company

www.myjones.com

Personalized bottles of soda

My Own Labels

45 NE Hancock Street

Portland, OR 97212

www.myownlabels.com

Fax: 503-295-2716

Many varieties of labels, including hangtags, CD labels, and food and wine labels

Oriental Trading Company

www.orientaltradingcompany.com

800-875-8480

Party supplies including miniature maracas, colorful glass bottles, coconut shells, and favor packaging

Pantry Press

103 Roncesvalles Avenue

Toronto, ON M6R 2K9

Canada

www.pantrypress.net

800-511-4767

Custom stationery

Paper Source

www.paper-source.com

888-PAPER-11 (888-727-3711)

Custom stationery, printed paper, envelopes, cards, hangtags

Photo Booth Rentals

www.photoboothrentals.com

888-634-6323

Old-fashioned black-and-white or color photo booths for rent in California

Photo-Me

1123 W. N. Carrier Parkway

Grand Prairie, TX 75050

www.photobooth.cjb.net

866-PHOTO-ME (866-746-8663)

Nationwide rentals of photo booths

Pressed Flower Gallery

1405 San Marino Avenue #100A

San Marino, CA 91108

www.pressedflower.com

626-795-6669

Pressed flowers for stationery and other uses

Saeyoung Vu Couture

www.VuCouture.com

Simple elegant dresses

Valerie Confections

www.valerieconfections.com

888-706-1408

Handmade toffees

Voss Water

900 Broadway

Suite 1003

New York, NY 10003

www.vosswater.com

212-995-2255

Bottles of Voss water for welcome bags

Wedding Things

#101-326 East Kent Avenue South

Vancouver, BC V5X 4N6

Canada

www.weddingthings.com

888-338-8818

Wedding gifts, favors, and packaging

West Elm

www.westelm.com

866-WESTELM (866-937-8356)

Vases, pillows, and other accessories

World Wide Chocolate

www.worldwidechocolate.com

800-664-9410

Online retailer of top-quality chocolates, including

Lindt chocolate balls and many others

index

Underscored page references indicate sidebars. **Boldface** references indicate photographs.